··· — ···

MINDFULNESS
for EMERGING ADULTS

Finding balance, belonging, focus, and meaning in the digital age

....

DONNA TORNEY
MA, LMHC, RYT

··· ——— ··· ———

WholePerson
Mental Health & We
publisher of therapy, counseling, and self-help
Duluth, Minnesota

T0051436

WholePerson
Mental Health & Wellness
publisher of therapy, counseling, and self-help resources

101 West 2nd Street, Suite 203
Duluth, MN 55802

800-247-6789

Books@WholePerson.com
WholePerson.com

Mindfulness for Emerging Adults
Finding balance, belonging, focus and meaning in the digital age

10 9 8 7 6 5 4 3 2 1

Editor: Peg Johnson
Art Director: Mathew Pawlak
Cover Design: Brett Fitzgerald

Library of Congress Control Number: 2017948006
ISBN:978-1 57025-353-9

——————————— ··· — ··· ———————————

Why we need *Mindfulness for Emerging Adults* in the digital age

Just as it is a toddler's developmental task to master walking and talking, it is the developmental task of emerging adults (young adults roughly 18 to 33 years old) to build independence and intimacy. However, if we want these emerging adults to truly thrive in our society, we need to go beyond the developmental basics. We know toddlers need to feel loved and safe for optimum development to occur, but we sometimes forget that emerging adults need to be resilient, compassionate, optimistic, and connected to community to reach their full potential.

Mindfulness for Emerging Adults explores the task of becoming an adult in the twenty-first century by citing advances in neuroscience to encourage seeing mindfulness and other contemplative practices as indispensable life skills. These ancient and now rigorously researched practices are more important than ever in our age of accelerated change, media overload, and chronic busyness. Due to the large interest in mindfulness by the scientific community, we now have evidence that these practices create positive change in the mind and body. By exploring and adopting mindfulness and other contemplative practices which I call *Center Points,* emerging adults can forge a path to find authentic identity and healthy personal and community connections, creating a good life in the digital age.

Part I presents an overview of emerging adult rites of passage, past and present. **Part II** briefly reviews the fields of study that inspired *Mindfulness for Emerging Adults,* including developmental psychology, positive psychology, neuroscience and the Eastern traditions from which modern mindfulness practices emerge.

Exploration of this material will build motivation to learn mindfulness and other contemplative practices. These skills can balance stress and build confidence in everyday young adult life.

In **Part III** readers will find a practical manual that provides a series of *Center Points* exercises broken down into four important categories: Balance, Belonging, Focus, and Meaning. Each category comprises a separate chapter that will enable readers to build a personalized toolbox of skills. These skills will empower emerging adults to take control of stress and navigate difficult emotions. By practicing the *Center Points* exercises, the occurrence of both positive emotion and action will increase. Both young adults and their mentors will become more grounded in the present moment and experience more ease, contentment, and life satisfaction – a state that positive psychologists refer to as well-being. From this place of growing comfort and ease, young adults will become more discerning and forward thinking, ready to take on the challenges of emerging adulthood with youthful common sense.

Throughout the book, highlighted sections entitled *Voices of Emerging Adults* tell the stories of typical young adult struggles. These stories are composites of tales I hear in my private therapy practice, with details changed to protect privacy. The most common themes are highlighted, such as finding intimacy in a digital world, managing debt, finding a fruitful and worthwhile career path, managing difficult emotions, and practicing self-care. Of course, maturity and growth most often happen outside of a therapist's office. One of the goals of *Mindfulness for Emerging Adults* is to help young adults identify mentors in different areas of their lives.

Highlighted sections entitled *Thoughts for Mentors* will guide older adults to better relate to young adult challenges. By listening to the voices of modern young adults and comparing their stories to the timeless developmental challenges of past generations, readers will be able to build greater understanding of the perennial journey to adulthood.

Even with the best set of tools, setbacks are a normal part of the human experience. These situations can cause us to lose sight of our identity and confidence in our abilities. Knowing where to turn in times of crisis is an important life skill. *Appendix A* provides an overview of resources, both traditional and mindfulness-based to help emerging adults recover from setbacks.

It is the nature of the human brain to worry and to look vigilantly for what might cause us unhappiness, rejection, or harm. This is especially true during times of transition. However, this tendency can be tamed. If you are a young adult reading *Mindfulness for Emerging Adults* you will see that you are not alone in your struggles to manage these tendencies. If you are a parent, teacher, counselor, or a mentor of young adults, you will have a chance to remember your own young adult experience, which will help you to see eye-to-eye with the emerging adults in your life. Above all, *Mindfulness for Emerging Adults* will inspire hope in young adults looking for the good life. Hopeful, compassionate, confident young adults will lead us to the best version of the twenty-first century.

"It takes more courage to examine the dark corners of your own soul than it does for a soldier to fight on a battlefield."
— W. B. Yeats

Thank you for your bravery!

Universally and eternally emerging adulthood is a transition time full of excitement and potential as well as risks and challenges. Facing our fears during times of transition is brave work. It may seem counterintuitive, but staying open-hearted and open-minded during the rollercoaster ride to adulthood gives us an opportunity to employ values-based decision making that will lead to balance, connection, and contentment.

DEDICATION

——————————— ··· — ··· ———————————

In memory of Donny Dickson
and wild things everywhere.

The creation of the *Center Points* model was inspired by the courageous young adults I work with who are trying to find their own definition of a good adult life; and by the parents, teachers, therapists, and other mentors who wholeheartedly want the best for the young adults in their lives. My hope is that *Mindfulness for Emerging Adults* will help young adults find their footing faster, avoiding some of the pitfalls of the first years of adulthood, moving toward a satisfying life, while growing the ability and desire to give back to their community.

——————————— ··· ——————————— ··· ———————————

Acknowledgments

My heartfelt thanks to the team at Whole Person Associates for helping me express the needs of the generations of adults emerging in a time of great cultural change. Peg Johnson, you are the mentor I've always dreamed of! Thank you. For the love and devotion of my husband, Ian Torney, for reassuring the timid young adult who still dwells inside. May we have a long life together filled with nature, art, and community. Greatest love and thanks to my children: Forrest and Hannah, my two emerging adults and first mindfulness teachers, and to Willy and Christian, my rising young adults. Love and luck to my niece, Kayleigh the brave and brilliant, and to my nephew Joey and his wife Cassie, and your solid young family. May you all thrive in our new fast-paced world of technology…the Age of Acceleration. I'd also like to thank friends who continue to help me find balance, belonging, focus and meaning, including Catherine Cahill, my soul sister; Becca Brewster, comrade in yoga and recovery; Lisa White, for teaching me the lingo of the publishing world; Laurie and Doug Dickson, from Manch-Vegas and beyond; Lisa Gold, for all the brainstorming sessions and clinical advice; Tricia and Matt Soule, for unconditional acceptance; and Catherine Parker, for encouraging me to, "Surround myself with good people." Friends and family, I'm grateful that we continue to come in and out of each other's busy lives. Thanks so much for your authenticity and for helping me see, in community, what I couldn't possibly see on my own.

TABLE OF CONTENTS

··· — ···

Part III– How to build a personalized toolbox of contemplative practices

—————————— ... —————————— ... ——————————

PART I

Maturity Then and Now

What comes to mind when you think of someone in early adulthood? Which young adult life lessons do you see as necessary rights of passage? As for the current generation, what life passages set them apart? In the next two chapters, we will seek to recognize what is common across generations to normalize the experience of emerging adulthood. We will be better able to connect across generations and normalize the human experience. Connecting with others' experience is an essential part of building community, and one of the outcomes of mindfulness practices. By reading through Part I, you will be able to approach your mentor, parent, boss, or new employee with greater understanding.

CHAPTER 1

Some Things Never Change:
The timeless story of emerging adulthood

What is emerging adulthood?

Beatniks in the '50s, hippies and protesters in the '60s, disco kings and queens of the '70's, the '80's young Wall Street banker, the '90's grunge scene, the millennial hipster. The physical trappings and the timing of adulthood are constantly changing, but the psychosocial aspirations remain the same.

Young adulthood has always been a time of intense transition and therefore a time of vulnerability and opportunity. Coming up with a standard definition of "emerging adulthood" can be tricky. In the United States lawmakers have defined adulthood in many ways. Eighteen is sufficient for voting and signing up for Selective Service yet alcohol purchase is not legal until age 21. In some cases, much younger teens are tried and sentenced as adults in our legal system.

Somewhere between the legal ramifications and the more lofty ideas of achieving happiness in young adulthood we can see universal patterns. We can also see critical points in history during which the road to adulthood was especially rocky. The time we are in now, the first decades of the twenty-first century with its historic and accelerated change is one such critical point.

Listen to the voices of emerging adults

The optimistic voices:

- I'm ready for a new adventure.
- I feel like I have a few good choices for my next move.
- I'm starting to feel like I have control over my daily schedule.
- I'm excited about my new friends.

The ambivalent voices:

- I'm not sure about the relationship I'm in.
- Online dating is such a chore.
- What's the point of going into so much debt with student loans if I can't get a job when I graduate?

The overwhelmed voices:

- It's impossible to live on what I make.
- I'm so stressed lately!
- Nothing seems to be going the way I thought it would.
- I can't meet people in this city.

The paralyzed voices:

- I feel so left out when I look at social media.
- I'm struggling to stay motivated.
- Asking for help seems like a weakness.
- Some of my coping skills are turning into bad habits...I'm so ashamed.
- I think I would feel more motivated if I felt connected to something or someone.

If you are an emerging adult you can probably relate to some of the above voices. Which category(ies) do you fall under? Rest assured that you are not alone in experiencing these emotions. If you're an older adult or mentor, you may know a young adult who is struggling to achieve independence and intimacy – the competing developmental goals of emerging adulthood – and you might be reminded of your own struggles to emerge fully from adolescence. In Part III, emerging adults learn how mindfulness and other scientifically proven and time-tested contemplative practices can balance the stressors of modern living. Through these practices we can find the perfect balance between the many benefits of the digital age and our human physiological needs that move at a much slower pace than most of the technology we use today. By practicing the *Center Points* exercises, emerging adults can create their unique definition of what positive psychologists call the good life – a life that highlights personal strengths and is aligned with personal values (rather than a parent's or mentor's strengths and values).

Using positive psychology and mindfulness to create a good life

Positive psychology focuses on the causes of health and overall well-being. Positive psychology theorists study factors such as personal strengths and values and look at the components of a healthy community. The result is a better understanding of how individuals can obtain gratification in the major life domains of work and love. The language of positive psychology can help us envision an emerging adult who is capitalizing on personal strengths and enjoying life, even in the face of challenges. We can picture an emerging adult following his or her unique path, choosing behaviors that lead to independence and promote well-being.

This healthy type of adult development is best achieved in a community – a social network that includes both online and face-to-face connections. At the same time, it requires thoughtful individual examination. Mindfulness, or purposefully paying attention to moment-to-moment experience without judgment, is a fantastic aid in the process of exploring values and identifying strengths, as well as increasing the rich direct experiences of everyday life. Engaging in practical mindfulness in this way leads to

13

more contentment and calm, whether you are young or old, paying bills or socializing.

Eastern and Western philosophers and social scientists have been asking questions about adult development for centuries in an attempt to find the magic formula for happiness. In modern life mass-marketed materialistic ideas of happiness sometimes override less fickle definitions of happiness, like well-being. We may be led to believe that more material possessions will lead to more happiness. But anyone who has felt the rush of leaving their favorite store, with shopping bags in hand, only to feel the rush wear off rather rapidly has taken a stroll on the hedonic treadmill that keeps us chasing the next pleasure. Positive psychologists and mindfulness practitioners take a broader, more realistic view of adult happiness, working to categorize universal values, personal strengths, and healthy community. These categories help in distinguishing between lasting joy and fleeting happiness.

The study of emerging adulthood

In recent years emerging adults have received a good deal of attention from social scientists and the popular press, resurrecting old questions about overall adult development. Sociologists have traditionally looked to the Big Five Milestones as a means to measure adulthood. They are:

1. Finishing one's education
2. Moving out of a parent's home
3. Getting a job
4. Getting married
5. Having a child

In 1960, 77% of women and 65% of men had obtained these milestones by age 30. By 2000, only 46% of women and 31% of men had obtained the Big Five. This is such a drastic change that demographers no longer use this data set to measure adulthood. So how do we measure maturity in the twenty-first century?

An updated definition of healthy emerging adulthood

Understanding that emerging adulthood is a distinct phase of life, exploring some of the enduring markers of this phase of life, and becoming familiar with recent breakthroughs in neuroscience that pertain to the young adult brain, will help emerging adults better understand themselves and their peers. The better we understand ourselves – our strengths and values – the easier it is for us to move toward health and happiness and to stay balanced.

Luckily for today's adults, the concept of emerging adulthood is now a solid field of study. Jeffrey Jensen Arnett, PhD, a developmental psychologist based at Clark University in Worcester, Massachusetts, is one of the pioneers in this field of study. According to Arnett's research, emerging adulthood exists whenever there is a gap of at least a few years between completing secondary school and finding established roles in society, such as steady work and stable community. The path from adolescence to fully formed adult is most decidedly expanded in our current culture. This is in part due to the fact that our knowledge-based, tech-based economy requires more training before most young adults can achieve economic security.

If the Big Five criteria are now outdated, when and how do we proclaim that an emerging adult has become a bona fide adult? Arnett's polls show that we now define mature adults as:
1. Taking responsibility for their own actions
2. Making independent decisions
3. Achieving financial independence

Thoughts for mentors:

Do you agree with the new criteria for reaching adulthood? Discuss these criteria with a young adult that you work with. As we will see, these new criteria do not come all at once, and there are many ways to become an independent adult. Although emerging adulthood is a distinct phase, reaching adulthood has many paths. Furthermore, the new milestones might define adulthood but do they define adult well-being? In the *Center Points* model we expand the definition of reaching adulthood to include well-being.

Center Points model of healthy young adulthood

Emerging adults will be working toward well-being when they:

1. Know how to ask for help when facing physical and emotional imbalances
2. Have at least one trusted confidant to call upon when coping with stress, moving toward building a network of support
3. Are actively seeking employment that utilizes personal strengths and sustains basic needs
4. Are actively working to define *personal* values that bring contentment and joy and are expressing these values in work and in love (important personal relationships)
5. Are experimenting with mature coping styles, and minimizing use of immature coping styles
6. Have a healthy awareness of the consequences of their actions and can practice impulse control

Thoughts for mentors:
Plant seeds, but first remember your own young self

I can clearly remember what it felt like to be twenty-four. If you can't, I'd suggest you take a few moments and put yourself back into a scene from your emerging adult life. Use all your senses for this exercise. What are you wearing? Are you with friends? Family members? Alone? Think about your surroundings and recall colors, aromas, and sounds. What was the soundtrack of your young adulthood? Here's what I remember:

I remember walking around my college campus, not sure where to go. My situation with my roommates was not going well. They seemed so much more sophisticated than I was. I was the only first-generation college student in the bunch. I wanted to feel as carefree as they seemed. At the same time, there was just a little too much partying going on for me. I was desperate to have some time alone. But where? In a cubicle in the library? I just didn't feel like I really belonged anywhere. I'm not sure if I was aware of it back then, but now I can see how that feeling made me too dependent on my boyfriend.

My experience wasn't all bad though. In my second year I made some good friends at my work-study job, and going on weekend trips with the Mountaineering Club led me away from the party scene and back into nature. Some of these experiences helped me to make real connections and start to get to know the real, young adult me.

When you think of your own young adulthood remember the urgency of your needs: to connect or to disengage from a relationship, to figure out what kind of work you wanted to do, or to simply figure out how to pay your bills. If you could go back in time and be your own mentor, what three seeds of wisdom would you plant? What three pieces of advice and encouragement would you give to your younger self to think about?

Planting seeds may sound like this:

- It's okay to feel lonely sometimes. I remember feeling that way at your age. It is painful but it will pass.
- Although loneliness can be uncomfortable, being in an unhealthy relationship can be even more uncomfortable. Be mindful of your craving for a relationship. Don't let it take over your decision-making and put you in an unhealthy situation.
- If you could choose any career what would it be? Right now is a good time for you to try out a few different options.

Mentors plant seeds. Notice the examples above focus on shared, universal emerging adult experiences like wanting to belong or wanting to be independent. Planting seeds involves:

- Listening and refraining from judgment
- Being more of a compassionate consultant, and less of a savior
- Dropping assumptions and keeping an open mind
- Practicing equanimity – staying calm and avoiding strong reactions
- Practicing compassion – managing your own distress in the presence of another's distress

Mentors are not perfect people or saints. In fact, you

may only be one or two steps ahead of your mentees. Remembering your own young self when you are helping an emerging adult, staying interested, open-minded, and planting seeds as opposed to fixing problems will make you more effective in your role as a mentor. Make this your motto: *I will be the person I needed when I was younger!*

——————— ··· ——————— ··· ———————

Isabel's story highlights typical struggles that twenty-first century young adults must work through. The stories presented throughout the book in Voices of Emerging Adults segments are composite stories representing common themes from my private therapy practice, with details changed to protect privacy.

——————— ··· — ··· ———————

Voices of Emerging Adults:
Isabel's Set-back

I have got to find a way to get out of here. This is not where I pictured myself at age twenty-two. I know I'm not the only person in my friend group to have to move back home to save up some cash but I feel like I'm in purgatory. I thought I was going to be able to make it work, living with two friends from high school and holding down two jobs this summer. It was really fun, actually, but Jess went back to school and Laura and I couldn't swing the rent. It's so hard living at home after having been out on my own. I have zero privacy and my parents are scrutinizing my every move. Every day we have less patience with each other. Today my father actually put a schedule up telling me when I'm allowed to use the washer and dryer. It's like a police state. I tried to tell him how hard it was to lose my independence. He half-jokingly said, "It's hard for me, too." I used to like my dad's sense of humor, but that comment really stung.

I really needed to Skype my college roommate for a while after that episode with dad. I had two good semesters at college,

19

but I just got so overwhelmed with the tuition bills and I started second-guessing my major. So I took a leave of absence and took the two jobs. Since that didn't work out, I'm having trouble staying positive. I know I should be doing more than applying for jobs online, but I just can't get myself to actually go and talk to people.

It was my college roommate who talked me into counseling. The stress of keeping her grades up to keep her scholarship was really weighing her down last year. She said talking to a college counselor was really helpful.

When I first met with my counselor, I was doing a great acting job by being super-agreeable. It just seemed like another sign of my failure, sitting in that office, so I kind of wanted to keep my misery to myself. But after the third session, I could tell she wasn't reacting to me the way my parents would if I told them how worried and lost I feel right now. She told me that setbacks are a normal part of young-adulthood. She didn't freak out when I told her I slept until noon yesterday. I liked the way she was trying to get me to see asking for help as a strength instead of weakness.

I guess I'll keep going for a while. Still, I'm really having a hard time believing that things will get better. My energy just keeps dwindling. I wonder what the counselor would say if I told her how isolated I really feel? I was always kind of the quiet one in my group of friends in high school. I thought I was growing out of it. Now I can't even seem to bring myself to go for a run without feeling self-conscious. I know I feel better when I get outside, but I really just want to curl up in my bed, or numb out on Netflix. I know it's not getting me anywhere to binge watch tv but at least it's an inexpensive break from the stress.

——————— ⋯ ——————— ⋯ ———————

What we can't get from technology – why emerging adults need contemplative practices now

Technology is wonderful! I am after all writing this book on my laptop, on a program that helps me catch typos and make my points as clearly as possible. However, the pervasiveness of technology can trick us into thinking that we are *physically* evolving just as rapidly as our digital gadgets. We are much more than walking, talking, processing systems. Our physiology is the same as our grandparents and our great-great-grandparents. The human nervous system we all possess needs to be cared for and tended to with connection to community and the natural world. Imagine you have zero connection to other humans and zero connection to nature. Lonely and terrifying, isn't it? You will start to understand the important role these connections play in our overall well-being. Direct experience (present-moment experience that employs use of the senses) as opposed to narrative experience (where we are planning or remembering) is the perfect complement to our tech-focused world. Direct experience is a main theme and mindfulness skill in the *Center Points* model.

Encouraging direct experience – the very center of *Center Points*

Take a moment to look out a window, finding a horizon if you can (studies show that gazing at a horizon lifts our mood) or gaze at an object right in front of you. Take a few deep breaths… relax your jaw and drop your shoulders. Call upon all your senses to directly experience the object of your gaze. Get specific about colors, shades, and shapes. Now expand your awareness to the space around the object. Add the senses of sound and scent to further observe the object. Depending on where you are and what you are doing you might even be able to employ the senses of taste and touch. Observe the object without any strong judgment. Take another deep breath. Notice the change in your level of calm.

You have just sampled what Buddhist teachings and neuroscientists sometimes call direct experience – using your senses to take in information coming to you in the present moment, without the filter of remembered or imagined experience. Direct experience is a feeling that nothing is between you and the object you are observing. Direct experience gives us the opportunity to see an object, a place, or even a person just as they are, as if seen for the first time. We feel a sense of connection to the present moment engendering a feeling of being calm and alert, yet relaxed.

Although technology has many benefits, it is difficult to cultivate an understanding of direct experience through our laptops and smartphones. Contemplative practices like direct experience and others introduced in Part III are the perfect counter-balance to the overuse of technology. These practices can help us get the most out of the high-tech, knowledge-based world in which we currently live. You will build a personalized tool box that will help you tap into direct experience on a daily basis. You will build the capacity to reset your nervous system in times of stress, connect with peers in a meaningful way, and follow through with important life goals. The great news is that these tools are free, are backed by scientific research, and don't require a big time commitment.

The *Center Points* exercises

The tools that foster emerging adult well-being are knowing when to ask for help, perusing right livelihood, using mature coping styles, and beginning to define personal values. These tools can be developed by working through the practices in Part III of *Mindfulness for Emerging Adults*. The four main categories in the *Center Points* exercises build a road map for achieving the new markers of adulthood.

The *Center Points*: Balance, Belonging, Focus, and Meaning

Balance – This *Center Points* domain cultivates harmony in the physical body and structural brain. The balancing exercises encourage emerging adults to build an awareness of how imbalances caused by inattention to basic needs and daily rhythms will ultimately impact their ability to build confidence, identity, and healthy connections. Practitioners of Eastern philosophies such as yoga and Buddhism might call this sense of balanced moderation equanimity.

Belonging – True intimacy requires building a sense of personal safety and attunement to the needs of self and others. The belonging exercises will help emerging adults feel grounded in their internal and external surroundings, even if the external surroundings are in a state of flux, enabling young adults to feel safe enough to start forging healthy connections. Compassion for self and others, a central principle in Eastern contemplative philosophies and now being studied by Western neuroscientists, is one of the keys to feeling a sense of belonging.

Focus – These exercises include time-honored and scientifically validated mindfulness-based exercises that will foster a calm, clear mind and more flexibility with emotional states. They are presented in terms that are easy to implement and relevant to the daily lives of emerging adults. Over time these exercises change the structure of the brain, fostering a greater sense of ease when facing daily life challenges. New studies show that those who meditate regularly have a thicker prefrontal cortex – the area of the brain that controls executive function, emotional control, and builds empathy. These exercises help with reducing anger and resentment, and build loving-kindness.

Meaning – Many emerging adults are not in touch with their heart's deepest longings, and as a result, end up following scripted paths in relationships or careers and miss the opportunity to enjoy rewarding careers and genuine relationships. The meaning exercises are designed to help emerging adults make conscious decisions in major life domains like choosing career paths, friends, and partners. Eastern contemplative principles of acceptance and joy are explored in this domain.

Using mindfulness as a tool for positive human development

Center Points represent four essential elements of mindfulness. The power of these four principles is in their ability to cultivate emotion regulation in young adulthood, bringing about a sense self-mastery and resilience early in life. The *Center Points* exercises are designed to build a sense of normalcy around typical emerging adult challenges, halting counterproductive thoughts of shame and isolation.

Mindfulness has become a household word in popular culture causing some of us to see mindfulness as just another fad. But emerging adults can trust in mindfulness practices thanks to the large body of scientific evidence proving the benefits of this once esoteric idea. Recent studies have shown that mindfulness practices can help us manage stress and anxiety, better communicate with friends and co-workers, and build our ability to give and receive love and compassion. Chapter 4 includes a sampling of studies relevant to emerging adults.

Most researchers define mindfulness to include these two main components:

1. Mindfulness is the practice of bringing yourself back to the present moment, over and over. Our minds are wired to have a sometimes anxiety-provoking bias toward planning for the future or remembering the past. Mindfulness practices tame this bias.

2. Mindfulness is reacting to the present moment without judgment. Mindfulness practices help us build the capacity to be in the present moment without self-critisim and without bias.

One emerging adult I work with describes mindfulness as the ability to be with one's current set of circumstances without freaking out. She tells me that mini-mindfulness breaks at her workplace help her notice when she is having an automatic negative reaction to a situation, something that was getting in the way of her success at work. By employing mindfulness she found that she was better able to stay open to present moment experience in a way that helps her feel less threatened by new people and places. This skill, in turn, helps her with making conscious choices about her future and building more successful connections with peers.

Positive psychology is another science that is growing in tandem with the science of mindfulness. Starting in the mid-20th century, in a time when millions of people were healing from the aftermath of two world wars, theories that elaborate on optimum human development began to emerge. These theories expanded on child development to acknowledge that adults continue to grow and evolve psychosocially way beyond the point of reaching full physical maturity. But this perpetual maturing only happens if we are willing to continue learning from life experiences and adapt in healthy ways – a process that demands mindfulness.

Erikson's stages of psychosocial development

Erik Erikson's classic model of psychosocial development has been used as a framework for exploring human growth beyond childhood by many prominent social scientists. Erikson's model measures timeless developmental struggles and serves as a good framework when thinking about using contemplative exercises to foster positive adult maturity. Erikson went well beyond Freud's focus on unconscious drives, seeking to legitimize theories of human altruistic potential.

The famous Harvard-Grant Study of Adult Development uses many of Erikson's ideas. The Grant study followed a cohort of men who entered Harvard in the late 1930s, along with other less privileged young men. For over seventy-five years, this study has measured everything from blood pressure, to alcohol intake, to coping styles, and more recently, to brain activity. The study compares these measurements with the participant's satisfaction and success in work and in relationships. Researchers involved with this longitudinal study are still collecting data and refining its findings on test subjects who are now in their eighth decade of life.

An understanding of Erikson's stages and especially the idea of crisis resolution will help emerging adults and their mentors appreciate the value of using contemplative practices early in adult life.

Summary – Erikson's stages of psychosocial development

Life stage	Conflict	Resolution or value attained	Manifestation in adult life	Example
Infancy (0-1 year)	Learning basic trust vs. mistrust	Hope	Appreciation of human interdependence	I accept help and trust that it is available.
Early childhood (1-3 years)	Autonomy vs. shame and doubt	Will	Acceptance of the life cycle and impermanence	I can manage disappointment.
Play age (3-6 years)	Initiative vs. guilt	Purpose	Humor, resiliency, compassion	I don't take myself too seriously; I take time to enjoy life.
School age (6-12 years)	Industry vs. inferiority	Competence	Humility, accepting unfulfilled hopes	I have both strengths and weaknesses.
Adolescence (12-19 years)	Identity vs. role confusion	Fidelity	Merging of complex thought and emotions	I take both emotions and logic into account.
Early adulthood (20-25 years)	Intimacy vs. isolation	Love	Acceptance of the complexity of long-term relationships, openness, loving-kindness	I am willing to work to maintain important relationships.
Adulthood (26-64 years)	Generativity vs. stagnation	Care	Caring for others, empathy and concern	My life has more meaning when I care for my community.
Elderhood (65 + years)	Ego integrity vs. despair	Wisdom	A sense of identity and integrity that tempers physical limitations	I feel content and I accept the aging process.

Most scholars of human development see Erickson's stages as flexible, to be expanded or contracted based on current cultural norms. They are not necessarily completed fully and sequentially.

As balance is gained in one area of psychosocial development, it will affect the next area. This is good news! Life presents many twists and turns and often we must abandon straight-forward developmental maturity in order to survive. The beauty of Erikson's model is that it acknowledges that individuals can circle back and revisit certain developmental processes.

Because of the current elongated road to adulthood, there is often a blending, some might say a clash, of the adolescent and emerging adult developmental milestones of finding identity and finding intimacy. George Vaillant, long-time director of the Harvard-Grant study, states that we must first master identity before finding true intimacy. Vaillant defines mastery of identity as achieving economic, social, and ideological independence from one's parents.

The reality of modern young adulthood

Most of the young adults I work with are not willing to hold off on searching for intimacy before obtaining a solid identity or complete economic independence. Here is where the *Center Points* exercises can be immensely helpful, in that they allow emerging adults to establish a working identity, or a work-in-progress identity, that also allows for a healthy exploration of intimacy. Vaillant acknowledges that even some members of the privileged Harvard cohort struggled half their lives to find identity. He offers at least one compelling example of a young man who lost his way and seemed to have found it when he was offered a period of contemplation and a chance to experience compassion and intimacy.

--- ··· — ··· ---

Voices of Emerging Adults

In his book, "Triumphs of Experience," a summary of the findings of the Harvard Study of Adult Development, George Vaillant tells the story of subject Godfrey Camille whose young adulthood in the 1930's and '40's illustrates the eternal struggle to find identity and intimacy, and the healing power of contemplative practice. According to the Grant Study criteria Godfrey was predicted to struggle with the young adult developmental tasks of forming identity and intimacy.

Indeed he did. The product of well-to-do but neurotic parents, Godfrey was a frequent visitor to the college infirmary. He seemed unable to regulate his nervous system, which manifested itself in a myriad of physical complaints. Although he did not seem to learn how to love and make genuine connections in college, he did manage to serve in the military and graduate from medical school but found no passion or meaning in medicine. In spite of his successes in the military and at med school, at age thirty-two, he made a suicide attempt.

At age thirty-five he had a life-changing experience. Diagnosed with tuberculosis, he was forced to spend a year convalescing at a veterans hospital. During this year he learned to be cared for and to be caring. In essence, he went on a mandatory year-long retreat that provided contemplative time, rest, and connection. He told Grant Study researchers that this time transformed him. He went on to marry, have a family, and run a successful medical clinic. In a later interview he tells the Grant Study, "I've slowly learned to become comfortable, joyful, connected, and effective." His year of physical recovery included emotional recovery. His time in the hospital allowed him time to contemplate, heal, and practice the Center Points skills of finding Balance, Belonging, Focus, and Meaning.

--- ··· --- ··· ---

The happy fact of circling back in adult development

Godfrey's story also illustrates the spiraling nature of maturity and the happy fact that we can always circle back to address unfinished stages of psychosocial development. In my counseling practice I find that, depending on maturity level and life circumstances, it is sometimes helpful to think of someone approaching their mid-thirties and even forties as still falling in the young adult category in terms of identity formation and ability to make authentic connections.

--------------------------------- ... — ... ---------------------------------

Thoughts for mentors: Beware of stereotypes – generational and individual

At the beginning of this chapter I listed some stereotypes associated with different generations of emerging adults. However, outer trappings of young adulthood, like the current popularity of tattoos, are just that – outer trappings, and they reveal nothing more about us than our human need to belong. Think back to your own fashion sense as an emerging adult. Would you want anyone to label you based on the trends of the time?

Labels do more harm than good

A college dean speaks:
I really put my foot in my mouth when I started taking about millennial traits at the freshman orientation. Afterwards a couple of students came up to me and told me they were offended by my comments about helicopter parents and their kids. These particular students reminded me that they were

actually here on scholarship, and each worked two jobs this summer to be able to enroll.

A few small studies support the media representation that millennials are pampered, fragile, and narcissistic. Larger collections of data like the Pew Research Study on Millennials show that they actually have a higher level of concern for the environment and greater participation in community service than past generations. Values like leading a meaningful life, having strong friendships, and finding steady work, have remained the same when compared to Baby Boomers and Gen-Exers. When working with a group of emerging adults, conduct a mental scan for any implicit or explicit biases you may be harboring. Then practice staying open-minded and inquisitive – two mindfulness skills that help with truly understanding and helping the young adult you are working with.

Individual stereotypes

A stepparent speaks.
Ever since I've known her (four years) Jill has always been impulsive. It's really hard for me to deal with. She's just always going to be self-centered.

Watch out for thoughts such as she's always been impulsive, or she's always going to be self-centered. You may be working with a young adult who is struggling with a behavior, even an addiction that is somehow keeping her stuck. Conduct a mental scan for any labels that may be forming about your emerging adult. Remember that they are still formulating enduring character traits.

——————————— ⋯ ——————————— ⋯ ———————————

The neuroscience of perennial maturation

Information made available via modern brain imaging can inform the neo-definition of adulthood. We now know that the human brain continues to develop and consolidate long after the teen years. Neuropsychologists have found that the frontal lobe region of the brain is not fully developed until our mid-twenties, and continues to grow for the rest of our lives.

It can be helpful to imagine the emerging adult brain and Erickson's developmental stages as a set of Russian nesting dolls. If one of the smaller dolls has a chip or a gap, it may not be able to fit easily into the next doll. It may require going back and reshaping the smaller doll for the entire set to fit. This is what Erikson meant when he suggested that circling back to resolve past developmental stages – going back, examining and resolving gaps – can bring about perpetual growth and life satisfaction.

Working through the *Center Points* exercises helps younger and older adults alike, to circle back, examine, and resolve any remaining role confusion left over from the previous stages of development. In essence the *Center Points* exercises use mindfulness as a tool to help with this process of developmental integration.

Consider Darcy's story:

―――――――――――――――― ··· — ··· ――――――――――――――――

Voices of Emerging Adults
Darcy: An opportunity to heal from and integrate life experience.

I'm just so disgusted with myself. I hate my body. I feel so awkward all the time. I guess I thought by studying women's issues, and getting a degree in psychology, I would find the strength to change my behavior. I thought my internship working with teen girls would change me. And yet here I am sitting in a therapist's waiting room, feeling like dirt.

I keep making horrible choices with guys. Logically, I understand now, that my relationship with my soccer coach was abusive. I get it. He was twenty-one, and I was only fifteen. I thought if I just kept having sex with him that he would really care about me. This was my first relationship, and I can see that it set me up to have a messed up view of intimacy. It messed with my self-esteem. I can see that. But what I don't understand, what horrifies me, is that I keep hooking up with guys I hardly know. They obviously don't care about me. At least I'm able to talk about it now with my friends. They are understanding and acceptance has really helped me.

I can't even picture myself in a healthy relationship. My therapist tells me that a healthy relationship takes time – that it takes time to build trust. I just don't think this applies to me. I don't think I deserve this. But something has to change. My panic attacks are getting worse. I meet somebody on Tinder, we hook up on the first date, and then I'm a wreck waiting for him to call back. When he doesn't, it just confirms my belief that I'm not worth it.

Today I need to tell my therapist that I've been drinking more and eating less. When I told her I get drunk before each date, she told me that we should work on changing that pattern, but I can't even imagine dating without drinking. I can't keep going in this direction. Last week I tried a different kind of on-line dating. The guy was older and he came to my apartment. We got drunk. When I woke up in the morning there was money on the bureau. I have never felt so low. I don't know what I was thinking. I feel so out of control.

—————————— ⋯ —————————— ⋯ ——————————

Experiences like Darcy's are unfortunately quite common, and while the circumstances have been made modern by the addition of the internet, this type of struggle to find healthy intimacy is timeless. We can view these events as developmental traumas. Big or small trauma during adolescence and young adulthood can shape behavior and the trajectory of life choices. It can keep us stuck in the crises of a developmental stage. Think of the damaged nesting doll that needs care.

Identity and the good life

With the help of contemplative practices, emerging adults like Darcy can heal from these developmental traumas and regain physiological and psychosocial balance. They can create a new and healthier definition of belonging. Contemplative exercise can also help emerging adults normalize seemingly debilitating experiences, dissolving the illusion of separateness and isolation they can bring, turning our struggles into proof of our resiliency and adding to a stronger sense of self.

The identity project: Encouraging mature coping styles

Early psychoanalytic thinkers defined common defense mechanisms, more frequently known as coping styles, that help individuals regulate emotions and reach goals. These defense mechanisms are often categorized as unhealthy, immature, and mature. The Harvard Men's Study found a strong correlation between the use of mature defense mechanisms, and triumphing over adversity in adult life. Buddhists and yogis may use the terms skillful or unskillful means, or mindfully healthy and unexamined unhealthy coping behaviors. Here's a partial list of defenses and coping styles classified as less skillful means and more skillful means along with an example of how they may show up in emerging adult life. As you read through the coping styles, can you remember using some of the less skillful coping styles? Is there a defense mechanism you still use that keeps you feeling isolated?

Less skillful means:

When the less skillful defense mechanisms are in use, we usually feel as though we have no control over our environment. These coping mechanisms are often semi-consciously employed. In an attempt to gain control, we might resort to these defenses. Unfortunately, they often create more chaos.

Less Skillful Defense Mechanism	Example
Aggression/Anger	An overly stressed and frustrated individual responds by punching a wall or person.
Denial	Ignoring the consequences of a dangerous behavior like unprotected sex, or binge drinking.
Displacement	Taking out frustrations from work on a family member.
Somatization	Mental stress and anxiety are ignored, but manifest as physical symptoms.
Dissociation	Mentally removing oneself from a stressful situation losing connection with people or physical surroundings.
Wishful thinking/ fantasy	Adopting an unrealistic view of a situation rather than facing disappointment.

More skillful means:

As we gain more life experience, we often learn more skillful coping mechanisms that help us feel more in control and capable of achieving independence and connectedness. At times we need mentors to help us move toward more skillful coping styles. In the example above, a person who is using denial and ignoring the consequences of heavy drinking might start to consider the more skillful means of moderation. Someone who is ignoring mental stress, but experiencing physical symptoms might identify with a friend who takes daily walks to manage stress and can start building his own awareness of the connection between mind and body.

More Skillful Defense Mechanism	Example
Moderation	A young adult who is struggling with spending too much time playing video games with friends decides to set a weekly time limit.
Patience/Acceptance	Instead of bringing frustrations from work into the home, a roommate decides to talk to her trainer at work .
Identification	Instead of letting unmanaged stress cause physical symptoms, a person in recovery identifies with the story of an ex-heroin addict who takes up running.
Sublimation/Altruism	Rather than feeling sad about not having a significant other, two single friends sign up to volunteer at a local charity .
Humor	Realizing that final exams are causing stress and low mood, a group of friends decides to watch a comedy on Netflix.
Anticipation	Foregoing a weekly dinner out to save for an upcoming vacation.
Suppression	Instead of lashing out and becoming consumed with a recent break-up a young musician waits until after an important performance to process the difficult emotions.

Normalizing the circling back process and filling in developmental gaps

The thread between Isabel, Godfrey, and Darcy's stories is the common story of a developmental gap keeping one stuck in less skillful means. Isabel is struggling with finding focus and meaning and resorting to the less skillful coping style of displacement and avoidance. Godfrey and Darcy, although their stories are vastly different and take place in different centuries, are both struggling with balance and belonging, but the less skillful coping skills of denial and somatization, are keeping them stuck.

Let's meet Jake, an emerging adult who has been using some less skillful coping styles.

··· — ···

Voices of Emerging Adults
Jake: Focusing and belonging

I thought I was doing a good job taking care of myself but my boss's comments at the end of my review were kind of a wakeup call. This time when I walk into her office I hope she notices that my clothes don't smell and I took a shower. I thought she was judging when she first brought it up, but I could tell she was just worried that I wasn't taking care of the basics, like scheduling in time to do laundry and eat. It's just so hard to focus lately.

The fights with Becca are getting worse. I have a stomachache almost all the time lately. I'm so jealous of any guy she talks to. Last night our fight was so bad that I hurt my fist by punching a wall. I hope I can still play at the show tonight.

I don't know what my problem is. I've been on my own since I was nineteen. I'm twenty-seven now. I always thought of myself as being super independent. So why am I so obsessive and crazy about my girlfriend? Sure, Becca and I are splitting expenses and it would be hard to live on my own. But at this point I'm ready to couch surf again. I know how to get by on almost nothing. That's how I was able to quit my job and tour with the band last year.

It's been a good thing to stop drinking and stay away from drugs. Last week my co-worker had me try some deep breathing exercises. They helped a little. We also talked about how much I used to like to mountain bike. I realized I'm hardly ever outside anymore. I'm trying to think of a way to get back into enjoying time on my own.

I'm still having a hard time sticking to my goals. Part
of me wants to apply to the community college for sound
engineering. Part of me just wants to take off and do another
tour, even though we hardly break – even financially when we
are on the road and the basics – like healthy food – take a hit.

——————————— ⋯ ——————————— ⋯ ———————————

Jake is typical of the many emerging adults looking for help
in finding intimate, meaningful relationships with friends and
romantic partners. However, Jake's coping style was lagging
behind his chronological age. Most emerging adults don't spend
a lot of time consciously thinking about their coping styles, in
fact in traditional psychoanalytic theory, defense mechanisms
are thought to be subconscious. The contemplative exercises in
Center Points will help emerging adults become more conscious of
unhealthy coping styles and move toward more skillful means of
managing stress.

——————————— ⋯ — ⋯ ———————————

Thoughts from mentors
Words from Jake's grandfather:

Imagine what it was like to be young 65 years
ago. It's hard for me to watch Jake struggle. But
when I was his age I was already a manager at the
paper mill, was married, and Jake's dad was on the way! It
wasn't easy but I can remember feeling proud. We had a
good group of neighbors – some stayed our neighbors for
fifty years! We didn't get our first television until 1960. It
seems every time Jake visits me he has a new gadget!

Sometimes I get frustrated with Jake. Those tattoos! And
I thought his dad was wild! I consider myself a modern
thinker. Hell, I have a tattoo from the Navy. It was just

our way of bonding. Even an old guy like me can see all the changes. I read the papers. I can see how hard it is for Jake's generation. I can also see how my wife may have been frustrated with being a housewife, raising three kids without access to a car every day. But it seems like Jake and his friends have fewer opportunities. We could buy a house on one income and easily pay it off on my manager's salary. Not so for Jake and his friends.

———————————— ... ———————————— ... ————————————

We are at a critical point of human evolution and cultural identity. We can look at the industrial revolution and imagine what it was like to be a young adult raised on a farm trying to make the transition to a more urban way of life. We can look at the Sixties and imagine what it was like for an emerging adult trying to make good decisions during a time of radical social change. We are again facing a sea change. The current knowledge-based, digital age is radically changing the way we live and think about ourselves in the world, not to mention the way we take care of our basic needs. There are many benefits to this new way of life, but as with any big cultural change, wise application of innovation can make the difference between a thoughtless, joyless existence and a life well-lived. Building balance, belonging, focus, and meaning early in life and facing direct experience with clarity will lead to healthy decision-making and healthy identity development for the individual and society. Speaking with elders like Jake's grandfather, looking back at past innovation and our adaptation to innovation will help us make wise choices with the newest wave of technology.

A flexible identity

Identity formation is a life-long process. A healthy, flexible identity can serve as a resting place, a place where we can practice direct experience with pleasure, or at least with less discomfort.

Like Erikson's theory, there are aspects of Buddhism and

39

yoga that foster healthy human development. Combining these aspects with newer theories in Western psychology such as positive psychology and modern neuroscience make these ancient practices accessible and practical for use in everyday young adult living.

Let's review one more story that illustrates the universal work of young adulthood with a modern spin. Some readers may think that Tracey's story sounds cliché. But the rules of finding intimacy have changed drastically due to online dating and digital overload. The idea that someone looks good on paper but is completely different in person is a real challenge for young adults. Furthermore, in the digital age, emerging adults are bombarded with images, many unrealistic, about what a healthy, happy relationship should look like.

--- ... — ... ---

Voices of Emerging Adults
Tracey – Balancing outside expectations with personal goals, and formulating a genuine identity.

I thought once Peter and I got engaged and I had a good first job that I would feel more confident. But lately I've been so anxious. That's why I decided to call Donna. I stayed home from work last Monday because I was overwhelmed with the wedding plans. I am trying to manage what my parents expect and what I really want. I just can't keep letting my emotions get the best of me!

I've also been kind of hiding from my friends. I don't understand why I can't let go of other people's standards and just live my own life. I have a great job and I just got a small raise. I'm just about the only one of my friends who can pay for an apartment and pay for my student loans. Why can't I just relax? Donna told me that I was sitting as still as a statue in our first session. The deep breathing has helped me relax a little and sleep better. I've stopped missing work but now I'm having doubts about Peter, which is really freaking me out!

I know everyone thinks we are the perfect couple. From the outside, everything looks ideal. We've been dating since sophomore year, and we are great friends. I really am a relationship person. I can't deal with the thought of going back to online dating. Plus almost all my friends are getting married now.

Donna asked me to do a couple of exercises to help me think about my strengths, and things I value. I realized that I never work on my art anymore! I used to love going to museums and taking art classes. In fact I was hoping I could add more design work into my job description.

It's just that Peter doesn't like art that much, and I really don't like doing things by myself. Like I said, I'm a very social person. I guess I really have been using this relationship to hide from my anxiety about being alone. Ugh! I can see now that the anxiety won't go away if I keep running away from it and trying to make everyone happy.

--------------------- ⋯ --------------------- ⋯ ---------------------

Craving/grasping and aversion/avoidance:

Tracey's anxiety is increasing at the same rate as her emerging craving to be able to express her true self. She has reached a point of such discomfort that she is willing to explore her coping styles. Without an honest exploration of true identity and personal values we are all susceptible to getting caught up in what Buddhists and yogis identify as the suffering of clinging to ideas at one extreme, and the unhappiness of avoidance of experience on the other.

Every generation of emerging adults has faced its own particular flavor of clinging and avoidance. For those reaching adulthood in the digital age clinging might show up as unhappily and hyper-vigilantly checking Facebook for status updates, or clinging to media-driven ideas of work, friendship, and family. Avoidance can manifest as a rigid and anxious stance against new ideas that might prevent exploring reasonable opportunities.

Summary:

As we can see from the four stories presented in this chapter, emerging adults are still striving to find healthy intimacy and authentic identity, just as past generations have done. The digital age and the accelerated pace of change along with associated sociocultural change can make it difficult to feel balanced and grounded. Yet some young adult rites of passage such as finding independence and intimacy remain the same across generations regardless of the current generational culture and norms. We will meet up with Isabel, Darcy, Jake, and Tracey again as we continue to explore the benefit of contemplative practices in reaching twenty-first century emerging adult goals and making the most out of the digital age.

CHAPTER 2

Some Things are Changing Rapidly:
Accelerated change and unique opportunities

"… People have bodies and souls, and when you feed one and not the other you always get in trouble. When people feel their identities and sense of home are being threatened, they will set aside economic interests and choose walls over Webs, and closed over open in a second.… In the age of accelerations, if society doesn't build floors under people, many will reach for a wall – no matter how self-defeating that would be.…"

— Thomas Friedman, *Thank You for Being Late*

The shaping of a generation

If you recently graduated from high school or college you are facing unique work opportunities and challenges. Forecasters are predicting that many of the job titles we will see in the next few decades have not yet been invented! How then, do young adults plan a future? Emerging adults can better manage this uncertainty when they are connected to peers who are experiencing similar challenges. Normalizing the emerging adult experience by connecting with others is a great stress reduction tool. However, for those who are overly stressed or feeling too defeated, it can be difficult to find the courage to connect.

—————————————— ··· — ··· ——————————————

Voices of Emerging Adults
Isabel's motivation reboot

I feel better now that I opened up to Donna about feeling like such a failure after moving back home. I've reconnected with an old friend from high school who is going through a similar situation. She thought for sure she wanted to be a lawyer, but she actually hated the coursework. I'm so glad I reached out to her when I saw her posts on Facebook.

It's funny; now that I feel less isolated I'm a little more motivated and a bit less stressed. I'm starting to plan my days out a little better so they have some kind of structure like when I was at school. Donna calls this having a social rhythm. I told her I was going to start a band called The Social Rhythms. I know I'm feeling better because my sense of humor is coming back.

I still have a long way to go though. It is really hard for me to get out of the house before 2 p.m. Donna suggested an exercise where I visualize a perfect day. It was really helpful! I can tell you that my perfect day does not include sleeping until noon, fighting with my parents, and hiding in my room with Netflix as my only companion! I mean, that might be okay over Christmas break, but as a daily occurrence it gets old quick! Since my perfect day involves socializing, I'm going to meet my old friend at Starbucks tomorrow. We are going to work on our resumes together.

—————————— ··· —————————— ··· ——————————

A community of supportive peers and mentors will help emerging adults feel exhilarated, not overwhelmed by the pace of change in the twenty-first century. Once our nervous systems are calmed by mindfully connecting with peers, we can turn our attention to the current cultural needs of the times, and match these needs with our personal values and strengths. We will explore values further in the exercises in Chapter 8. Let's first continue to explore the opportunities and challenges that define the modern emerging adult experience.

——————————————— ··· — ··· ———————————————

Thoughts for mentors:
Generations in the workplace

I've been a trainer at a large insurance company for almost twenty-five years. When I first saw new employees looking at their cell phones and laptops during meetings I just could not believe it! It felt so disrespectful! Luckily our Human Resources Director is well trained and up-to-date on how to best work with different generations in the workplace. She suggested I adopt the following ideas:

Consider the idea of mutual mentoring. Because new technology and the way we receive information is changing so rapidly, it's very possible that the emerging adult I'm training knows a lot more than I do about such topics as social media, and how it can promote products and keep communities connected. I've started asking young adult hires about how these changes affect them. They are truly the experts. This approach not only helps me better understand their world and be a more empathetic mentor; I've also been able to pass ideas along to our information technology department.

Be Respectful: HR suggested I talk to younger employees as if I were visiting a foreign country. After all, I wouldn't visit Japan and expect the locals to change their culture to suit me! I would try to understand why they approach life differently and get a sense of how we are the same.

Now I can better see how all the generations in the workplace are interdependent. This is true outside of the workplace too. It's not naturally apparent in the United States where we tend to keep the generations separate. A workplace study in France discovered mixed-generation work groups are more productive than single generation work groups. The different generations benefit in many ways by spending time together. We are more creative, more productive, and feel more connected when we embrace intergenerational teamwork. When HR told me about this study I decided we needed to create mixed-generation workgroups at our company. These groups have come up with some great ideas! The process has helped me remember that every generation appreciates people who are approachable and respectful. In truth, being empathetic is a good business skill.

_____ ⋯ _____ ⋯ _____

What we know about twenty-first century emerging adult life

The 2010 Pew Research Center report on Millennials sheds light on the world of the modern emerging adult. We can be sure that the next generation following in the footsteps of the Millennial generation will continue to be affected by accelerated change, as there is no sign the pace of change is slowing down. Luckily mindfulness and other contemplative practices allow us to slow down, no matter how fast our world seems to be spinning. In the following pages, you will find some research on the first group of young adults to emerge in the twenty-first century. As you read through the findings, keep in mind that statistics can contribute to generalizations, and that the current group of young adults still has a lot to show the world.

Mutual Mentoring

Emerging adults coming of age in the first part of the twenty-first century are in need of a unique form of mentorship. In fact, new data on Millennials in the workplace shows that this group appreciates frequent feedback from mentors. In his book, *Sticking Points* (2013) generational coach Haydn Shaw states that Millennials are open to mentorship from supervisors – more so than Baby Boomers and Gen-Xers were when they were young adults. Mutual mentoring, being curious and open-minded, embracing interdependence, and building empathy are all skills that can be cultivated through mindfulness practices. We can see from this finding that it is just as important for mentors to be mindful as it is for the emerging adults they are mentoring.

A Challenging Economy

What is a living wage these days? After adjusting for inflation, wages have been in a downward trajectory since 1970. In contrast, at the turn of the last century at the height of the industrial age, a young person could finish their high school education (or not) and with little or no further training, could rise up the ranks of a manufacturing-based business, and live a comfortable life – economically speaking. It now takes longer to find a secure place in society due to the need for more training and education. This may be one reason why many emerging adults see themselves as not reaching adulthood until their late twenties, and that the outdated criteria for reaching adulthood including buying a home and having children, simply seems out of reach.

Attitudes toward work and finances

Another common theme in the lives of twenty-first century emerging adults is financial overwhelm. Many emerging adults, even those with college degrees, work training, and good references and work experience are feeling the effects of a rapidly changing economy. With fewer jobs that offer a living wage, and/or mountains of student loans to repay, many emerging adults are just getting by financially and feel overwhelmed with daily life. Staying optimistic and hopeful about having a good life in this climate is a real challenge. Yet one of the traits of emerging adulthood, according to researcher Jeffrey Arnett, is a positive outlook and a sense that many possibilities lay ahead. Even so, The American Dream will look much different for this cohort than it did for the Baby Boomers and even Gen-Xers. Economist Robert Gordon is predicting that the tech revolution, as exciting and life changing as it is, will not translate into as many jobs as the industrial revolution did. On the same stage, however, MIT's Erik Brynjolfsson makes a more optimistic forecast predicting never before seen exponential growth. The jury is still out on technologies true effect on job growth.

--- ··· — ··· ---

Voices of Young Adults
Jake: Learning to manage typical adult stressors

I was really relieved when Donna suggested walking outside instead of sitting in her office for our session today. I got my bike out last week. It felt so good to go to the reservoir park and be in the woods. I realized this is one area of my life I have complete control over. Becca and I got along so well that night. She wants to rent a bike and come with me this weekend. The exercise helped me calm down enough to face my budget. I'm sold on more outdoor time!

Donna explained that exercise is one of the best ways to build focus. When you're a kid messing around on your mountain bike you don't think about these things — you're just in the moment having fun. But now I understand that getting my heart rate up changes the chemistry in my brain, waking me up, and calming me down. It's better than coffee! I just have to try to make it a habit. I'm motivated though, especially if it helps me control my stupid jealousy and my reactions. Even just walking around the block right now is helping me to feel better. It's like exercise is a moving mindfulness practice.

——————— ··· ——————— ··· ———————

——————— ··· — ··· ———————

Thoughts for mentors:
Does socioeconomic class make a difference?

I, for one, believe it does and asking about family socioeconomic background is a regular part of getting to know the young adults I work with in my counseling practice. Discussions about race and gender equality are ongoing in the US. However, discussions about the effect of socioeconomic class and the barriers created by income differences are not as conspicuous. I can't readily tell if a student I'm seeing who is attending Harvard is a legacy from a long line of Ivy Leaguers or a first-generation college student. It makes a huge difference in terms of sense of self for a lot of young adults.

Perhaps, because we are the "home of the free," and our Declaration of Independence states all men are created equal we find a discussion of class differences too uncomfortable. Even though it is getting more and more difficult to ignore the class divide, talking about money and income seems to be the last taboo. This generation is more realistic about the meaning of socioeconomic differences. There are real barriers that we can no longer ignore. Emerging adults from poor families have fewer safety nets. Middle class families find themselves making just enough money to pay the bills, but too much to obtain reasonable financial aid for higher education. These economic barriers can be overcome, but we as mentors need to allow and even facilitate space for emerging adults to talk about these differences, and how they affect self-concept, motivation, and hope.

——————————— ... ——————————— ... ———————————

The American ideal that if you work hard you can have it all does not ring true for many emerging adults. At the same time emerging adults are still being bombarded with ads that tell them that all they need is the newest expensive gadget to find happiness. This feeling of being a have-not in a must-have culture is, according to positive psychology research, one of the leading causes of unhappiness. It's believed to be one of the reasons that even though we are one of the most stable and richest countries on the planet, American life satisfaction is on the decline, and is even lower than citizens of some third-world countries (Graham, 2015).

In many ways this "it's out-of-my-reach" mindset is probably an eternal trait of young adulthood – perhaps a trait that spurs us on to greater achievements. Many older adults tell their stories of getting by on a shoestring with pride. However, this potential positive motivation can turn to hopelessness in the face of isolation, high student debt, or when the lack of gainful employment becomes a real barrier.

The gig culture: Moving from one short-term job to another with no expectation of permanence.

Some of the emerging adults I work with have complained about the gig culture. They feel that employers expect a lot from them, and yet they feel like a disposable resource. Emerging adults who are in lower paying entry-level jobs are often unable to afford health insurance. I have heard stories from emerging adults on the other end of the spectrum as well, those working for start-ups or high-tech companies that demand 50 plus hour workweeks. This group is struggling with finding a work/life balance. The knowledge economy and technology allow for 24/7 connections not only to friends and family, but to the workplace as well.

Young adults often come to my office having established unhealthy work habits that don't allow for exercise, rest, and recovery. It may be more critical than ever for emerging adults to practice good self-care since the research tells us that this generation is the least likely to be covered by health care, at least in the US. Emerging adults in their first professional position often have no idea about healthy boundaries and healthy levels of loyalty and respect. Here is where mentoring, coaching, and mindful communication can make a big difference.

_____ ... — ... _____

Voices of Emerging Adults:
Tracey: "What if I lose my edge?"

I still have some concerns about mindfulness. What if I lose my edge at work? I mean I have career goals. I don't want to become a slacker. Two of my co-workers came up with a great idea that really impressed my boss. Now I can't relax! I'm already falling behind with my career goals. I need to stay sharp to reach those goals. I'm afraid if I practice mindfulness I might be too relaxed and miss an opportunity.

But Donna reminded me that these practices are not just a new-age idea. I guess there is a mountain of evidence that shows that mindfulness and other stress-reduction exercises can help rewire your nervous system so you experience more frequent episodes of calm and clarity, and fewer episodes of stress and panic. I do feel like the practices helped me express my thoughts and feelings to my fiancé. I just can't picture how it will help me at work.

――――――― ... ――――――― ... ―――――――

Giving constructive feedback early and often, and treating younger employees as equals is essential for retaining emerging adults in the workplace. Keeping in mind that this generation struggles with a sense of isolation in spite of 24/7 connectivity, progressive employers are providing social connections, fun, and community on the job. Mentorship, respect, and a social connection go a long way in creating loyalty in the emerging adult cohort. Sharing *Center Points* exercises with emerging adults as a means to foster healthy decision-making, better communication, and a healthy work/life balance is an important learning experience – no student loans required!

――――――― ... — ... ―――――――

Voices of Emerging Adults

I am sitting in a coffee shop in Cambridge, Massachusetts when I overhear a conversation between two young women in their twenties, as they are simultaneously drinking their coffee, chatting with each other, and monitoring their smartphones. One of the two women is looking at her Facebook account and announces that she has been invited to a party that is to take place the next evening. The second young lady says, "Oh," and becomes rather rigid in her chair and then silently stares at her own phone. A few seconds later her phone pings, and, as if she is emerging from underwater, she gasps, "Oh, I just got the invitation too." I watch as her body language becomes much more relaxed.

――――――― ... ――――――― ... ―――――――

Finding a new definition of community

Twenty-first century emerging adults, just like young adults of previous generations, want to be part of a tribe. They want to belong to a close community of peers that help normalize their shared experience as they pass through the social and cultural initiations that give them access to adulthood. One striking difference with the twenty-first century emerging adults is that they use technology as the main glue for social cohesion. As the conversation in the coffee shop illustrates, this group sees technology as a necessary part of everyday life. The Pew Research poll found that 83% of Millennials sleep with their cell phone right next to their bed, as opposed to 68% of Gen-xers, 50% of Baby Boomers, and 20% of Traditionalists (Pew Research Center, 2010).

Staying connected at work is an important benefit for digital natives. Software giant Cisco reports that 56% of college students globally would turn down a job offer if the company prohibited use of social media (Shaw, 2013). There is no doubt that this generation has an intense relationship with technology, which plays an almost personified role in their lives, shaping the way emerging adults build community, build identity, and experience the world.

——————————————— ··· — ··· ———————————————

Thoughts from mentors:
A parent learns to respect new ways of communication

I keep hearing people tossing the term Luddite around. To tell you the truth, I had to Google it. Hah! If I used Google to find out what it means I guess that proves that I'm not a Luddite! My kids are using the term to describe an individual who can't or won't use modern technology. What I learned through my internet search is that the Luddites where a group of nineteenth century protestors who questioned the rising use of technology during the dawn of the industrial age. It turns out that the Luddites were not against the use of industrial age machinery. Their goal was to promote the proper use of technology. They wanted technology, which in their day included using powerful, sometimes-dangerous new machinery in factories, to be safe. They also wanted people to be aware of the way new technology changed the human heart and mind.

I've learned that one of the surest ways to lose the attention of any young adult is to completely disparage the use of technology. Comments such as, "Young people just expect a quick response to everything." or lamenting the cultural loss of cursive handwriting will most certainly bring about defensive eye-rolls, uncomfortable silences, if not outright hostility. I've found it to be interesting to talk to my daughter and her friends about how the digital age helps and hurts their friendships and work relationships. And there's been a lot less eye-rolling at dad lately!

———————————— ··· ———————————— ··· ————————————

Formal community support looks much different today than it did even twenty years ago. Opportunities to connect with nearby family, organized religion, and regular access to nature are cultural structures that have traditionally offered opportunities for centering, connection, and self-reflection. They are much less a prominent part of modern emerging adult life. We live in an increasingly mobile world, and the emerging adult cohort is especially mobile. Staying connected with family and friends electronically is an important way to fill the friendship/family gap. Problems arise, however, when emerging adults rely solely on digital sources and fail to make new connections through direct experience. I have had emerging adults describe a feeling of watching life from the sidelines when they do not have many opportunities for direct, in-person connection with their peers.

It's not just younger adults who are feeling isolated. Older adults are also feeling this change in community support, both because of the increased use of technology and our culture of busyness. Mindfulness around technology will help us capitalize on the benefits of the information age, such as universal access to learning opportunities, while helping us avoid the pitfalls, such as a decreasing sense of well-being because of a lack of community connection.

The mobile-global generation

Because of the elongated road to adulthood, there is more time to try on different hats. Loyalty and respect mean different things to different generations. Twenty-first century young adults will likely have many jobs if not careers during their work lives when compared to earlier generations. They are the first of four generations not to cite work ethic as a value, according to the Pew research. This does not mean they are not motivated, however. But they are far less likely than their baby boomer parents to overcommit to a particular institution, especially if they can't see their progression in the workplace as prior generations could. They are more likely to be wary of being loyal to a company that may not be around in a few years.

Emerging adults are also more likely to live further away from family. Distance from one's roots can be an exciting adventure but can also cause a sense of groundlessness. Managing groundlessness and uncertainty is one of the key themes in mindfulness practices.

——————————————— ··· — ··· ———————————————

Thoughts for mentors:
Disconnection to nature and self as part of nature

We are part of the natural world. I find that overstimulation is a real health risk in the modern era. Adults of all ages come to me complaining about diminishing down time. As a culture we no longer listen to our natural biological rhythms. Emerging adults, especially, fall prey to staring at the computer screen late into the night or keeping the ear buds in much of the day, as they are a generation that uses technology for social cohesion. This can be wonderful in moderation, until the accumulation of light and sound begin to interrupt sleep rhythms, leading to a cascade of mental and physical disruptions. This is a serious risk to well-being.

A crucial part of staying healthy in the twenty-first century is to remember that our nervous system has not caught up with the speed of cultural change. Respecting this fact, and building a personalized toolbox to stay physiologically balanced is the key to getting the most out of the digital age. By reading through the *Center Points* exercises, especially those in Chapter 5, you will learn how to stay connected to natural rhythms while enjoying the best that technology has to offer.

——————————————— ··· ——————————— ··· ———————————————

The unattached generation

Twenty-first century young adults are also delaying marriage and they may be more thoughtful and cautious about starting a family. More members of this generation than in past generations were raised in a single parent household. The Pew data tells us this group of emerging adults considers themselves to have strong family values. Perhaps the divorce rate is leading to more singlehood, or perhaps the narrowing of the wage gap is leading more young women to put off committed relationships.

Though single, many members of this generation are likely to have a roommate or two. Living alone and paying one's way is a real challenge in the current economic climate. For this reason, we are seeing more than double the number of Millennials returning home after leaving compared to their Gen-X counterparts. This generation like all generations past longs for connection, but their path to connection, community, and family is as unclear as the millennial career trajectory. Enter the *Center Points* exercises, to help twenty-first century young adults ward off isolation, and stay balanced and optimistic as they lead the way to new definitions of independence, intimacy and community.

―――――――――― ··· — ··· ――――――――――

Voices of Emerging Adults
Darcy – compassion inward

I'm starting to feel a little better than I did at our first appointment, after that terrible date where the guy left me money. I'm sad, but not as anxious as I was a few weeks ago. It's not like I feel sorry for myself exactly. It's more like I just want to cut myself some slack. My counselor didn't lecture me about giving up all my bad habits. Instead she asked me to do one thing a day that I would do for my best friend if she were in this situation. I decided I was going to try to eat three small meals a day instead of depriving myself. I've started sleeping a little better. The week before I added listening to a guided meditation on an app on my smartphone. It seems like those two small changes have helped me put the brakes on the dating websites for a while. Yes, I've had some moments of panic when I have a free night without plans, and I still wonder if I'll ever learn to accept kindness, but for now at least it feels good not to be adding to my pile of self-loathing.

My next assignment is to add a loving-kindness meditation where I start by extending loving-kindness to myself. The script goes like this:
May I be happy and safe.
May I have health in my body and mind.
May I have ease in my daily life.
May I be free from internal and external strife.

It just seems like such a foreign concept to me – being kind to myself. It actually makes me want to cry when I think about it. It also kind of feels selfish to focus on myself first. But Donna reminded me about the new research on self-compassion that shows it is a much better way to change behavior than self-recrimination. We are going to practice together in our next session and I also found a mindfulness group on campus. I know it will help to be with other grad students who want to find some stress relief.

I'm starting to realize I have a choice – that I can say no to these guys who were treating me the same way my first boyfriend did, that I deserved better, and this new behavior will free up my energy to help others. So I guess self-compassion isn't self-centered after all.

I know I'm not going to be able to change everything overnight. There's a big party this weekend. It's going to be hard not to slip into old behaviors. But right now, I feel so much more clear-headed and relaxed than I did a month ago. My friends have even noticed and they said they would support me at the party. I'm starting to have hope that I can live a different way.

—————————— ... —————————— ... ——————————

Values and social attitudes

The preliminary data provided by the Pew Research Center, paints a picture of a socially conscious generation that is open to new ideas, including new definitions of gender roles and family life. This generation is much more involved in non-profit work and more likely to volunteer than previous generations. They are also more likely to be accepting of homosexuality and transgender issues, and are more likely to have friends across the gender/sexual orientation spectrum. Many emerging adults identify as liberal, and are more accepting of racial diversity than previous generations. This generation has seen the number of women enrolled in college surpass that of men. The Pew research also reveals that men expect to have a spouse work outside the home. Both genders expect to share household and financial responsibility.

Why are contemplative practices so important now?

In short, contemplative exercises are an important offset for the life style changes brought about by the information age and the cultural reworking of definitions of community support and connection. A Pixar film called *Wall-E* released in 2008 helps illustrate the need for mindfulness and contemplative exercise in the modern era. The film takes place in the far-off future where humans are wheeled around in motorized carts. Every daily activity is automated, so there is very little need for muscle tissue. When the plot reveals a need to take action, Captain B. McCrea finds he has to learn how to walk the old-fashioned way, without a cart, like his earth-dwelling ancestors.

Because we have become a knowledge-based society we run the risk of treating ourselves like characters from the movie *Wall-E,* as if our minds are mere computer interface systems propped up on a pile of bones and muscle. Although technology affords many conveniences, it can also put emerging adults in a mindset where they begin to believe that they don't need a connection to the natural world, including contact with other human beings; that they are no longer of nature. Institutions that afforded time for contemplation, like organized religion are fading into the background. At the same time family support and close-knit community ties continue to disperse. We are a culture with an almost complete lack of ritual or observation of rites of passage; leaving no time to stop and think about the path we are traveling. Time to stop and think – it's not something that is valued in our digital, 24/7 society. However, advances in neuroscience have proven that a contemplative practice can help with creativity, balance, connection, productivity, flexibility, and decision-making – skills that are needed to succeed in the twenty-first century.

For many, young adulthood is a time for experiencing the disappointments that are inherent to being human. These setbacks – job changes, friend groups dispersing, a painful romantic break-up – can be derailing. Having a toolbox of contemplative practices can help emerging adults recover from painful experiences and integrate new lessons into their lives. At the same time, contemplative practices help young people absorb their successes in a way that will help them build confidence and joy, creating a positive cycle of good decision making. Because of the great technological, economic, and social sea change we are facing, we need practices that anchor us to the unavoidable reality of our human nervous system more than ever. Even though technology has changed the way we see the world dramatically, we are still social animals with physiological needs. The *Center Points* exercises present an outline to help emerging adults address those needs.

Staying hopeful

There is evidence to be hopeful about the mark the millennials will leave upon the world. The Pew Research Center data tells us that voter turnout of young people rose significantly in the 2008 and 2012 elections. Even so, only about 46% of eligible millennial voters actually went to the polls in 2016. They continued at the same level of participation as in 2012. In all three elections they made up 19% of the total number of those voting. Millennials are now a larger bloc of voters than baby boomers. Should they join together in support of an issue or candidate and exercise their political muscle, they will make an extraordinary mark on the politics of the nation. (Wisconsin Public Radio, 2016)

At any point in history, we can choose to look at the contributions of a generation, or how they detracted from society. Guidance and self-reflection can make the difference between a purposeful life and a life on autopilot for both older and younger adults. This is a timeless truth. To truly help emerging adults reach their potential, mentors themselves must reflect on the universal truths of human development so that both mentor and mentee can face opportunities and challenges with a calm, clear, unbiased mind. Mindfulness and other contemplative traditions help us understand our strengths and weaknesses. Through an exploration of timeless developmental challenges, and striving for authentic identity and connection, we can help each other make the most of our unique gifts.

———————————————— ··· — ··· ————————————————

Thoughts for mentors:
Are you the best mentor for the job?

I am constantly struck by the contrast of how rational I can be with emerging adults in my counseling practice and how completely irrational I can be with my own emerging adult children. Our own children's struggles can be just too painful to watch. Parents and guardians who have made it through the rugged task of launching emerging adults into the world will tell you that one of the best ways to teach the mindfulness skills of balance, belonging, focus, and meaning is to model these behaviors. That's why I encourage parents and mentors to also practice the *Center Points* exercises.

During mindfulness-based stress reduction trainings, including those designed for parents, participants learn about concepts such as letting go, beginner's mind (experiencing events with a fresh, non-biased attitude), non-striving, non-judgment, moderation, and equanimity. It is worth noting that the job of parenting is often hampered by questions that run counter to mindfulness, such as attachment issues (how tightly should my child cling to me?), family background (am I destined to repeat the patterns of my parents? am I ruled by my past?), future expectations (how much should I shape my children's future and how much of their future can I control?), and critical self-judgment (I should be a better parent). Parenting, in short, has strong potential to take us out of the here and now. Yet mindfulness research shows that the process of grounding oneself in the present moment allows us to access inner wisdom, thereby making better decisions and experiencing more life satisfaction and joy in parenting – even when parenting young adults.

Many concepts taught in mindfulness-based trainings are directly related to family resiliency, such as:

- Parenting self-efficacy – the belief in one's competency and effectiveness as a parent
- Open-mindedness – being curious about a situation as opposed to jumping to conclusions

- Non-attachment – staying unattached to an outcome
- Equanimity – evenness of mind, especially under pressure
- Right speech – using non-hurtful language
- Impermanence – fostering acceptance of changing family dynamics
- Yoga techniques – such as deep breathing and gentle stretching that support a non-reactive, calm nervous system

These are just a few of the tools that can be used to foster self-confidence and satisfaction in the challenging job of parenting and mentoring emerging adults. When I use these practices, I truly feel like the best person for the job of mentoring young adults.

——————————— ⋯ ——————————— ⋯ ———————————

Keep Neuroscience in Mind

Different data sets define each generational cohort differently. The *Mindfulness for Emerging Adults* definition of an emerging adult is based on neuroscience and developmental psychology. Recent discoveries in the field of neuroscience tell us that the brain is still pruning and refining itself well into the second decade of life. Developmental psychology tells us that circumstance can cause detours in the path to maturity.

New data on the brain calls us to rethink the way we view maturity, and how we view adult development. The good news is that we also know that mindfulness practices rewire the brain in such a way that greater flexibility in thinking and behavior is encouraged. The plasticity of the brain allows the gift of healing from stressful and traumatic experiences. What good news!

Flexibility, as it turns out, is just what is needed when surfing the ever-changing waters of twenty-first century work and relationship building.

Keep STEAMpathy in mind

The acronyms STEM and STEAM have become widely used in education in recent years. STEM, which stands for Science, Technology, Engineering, and Math, and STEAM, which adds Art Education to the mix, are terms used by progressive educators who advocate for a focus on these subjects in modern education. These are the tools that twenty-first century emerging adults need to possess in order to keep up with the rapidly developing innovations in the marketplace. In a New York Times article, Pulitzer Prize winning journalist Thomas L. Friedman adds empathy to the STEAM mix (Nov 2, 2016). He states, "The best jobs in the future are going to be what I call 'STEMpathy' jobs – Jobs that blend STEM skills with human empathy." The empathy piece will be needed, as there are jobs that no computer can replace, and comfort that no online interface can provide. Emerging adults will thrive if both they and their mentors build the flexibility to adapt quickly to change, and are willing to adopt STEAM as well as empathy skills. This combination of expertise will help emerging adults stay in the flow of change, both professionally and personally in the age of acceleration.

Summary

Today's generation of emerging adults are living a new way of life. Constant, accelerated change is unavoidable. The Digital Age offers a great deal including easy methods of staying in touch and connecting with peers to compare experiences. Millennials are curious, are open-minded, enjoy the interdependency of today's culture, are open to other lifestyles, and are tech-savvy. Mentors need to be aware of these traits and embrace them as well. Although working with earbuds in seems counterproductive and a bit rude to many mentors, emerging adults see those earbuds as the norm. Only if mentors make the effort to understand and embrace the good qualities of the world of emerging adults will they be able to connect with the people that use them.

Because so much of their interaction is digital instead of face-to-face, emerging adults will find that they sometimes feel isolated from each other and the rest of the world. They struggle with change because they have not yet learned coping mechanisms to help them put change in the right perspective. Mindfulness will teach them the skills they need, especially when we consider our need for balance, social belonging, focus and meaning. They will be able to come to a place of peace and review the alternatives from a new point of view.

In Part II we will take a look at two traditions from which our modern interest in mindfulness springs forth, along with an overview of some the latest research on mindfulness practices that is relevant to emerging adults.

Building Motivation to use Mindfulness as an Important Life Skill

Do you get more excited at the thought of reading historical novels, or non-fiction science writing? Are you more of an anthropologist, interested in making cross-cultural connections, or are you more interested in looking at fMRI scans of the human brain that show individual differences and similarities. In counseling sessions I find that some people are motivated to explore mindfulness exercises by learning about the history of various contemplative practices across the world. These individuals are often able to draw connections between Buddhist and yogic techniques for stress reduction and contemplative practices from their own culture. Other people would rather learn about the large body of scientific research that has amassed over the past 25 years. These studies show us that mindfulness helps with everything from healing trauma, to increased creativity, managing chronic illness, conflict management, increased experience of positive emotions, and care-giver stress.

The next two chapters take a brief look at both the wisdom traditions and the science as it relates to the developmental stage of emerging adulthood. By having an understanding of these two points of view you will be able to personalize your mindfulness practice and find fresh motivation to keep your practice alive, no matter what stage of life you're in.

CHAPTER 3

Models of Healthy Adult Development Found in Western and Eastern Contemplative Practices

"... the faculty of voluntarily bringing back a wandering attention, over and over again, is the very root of judgment, character, and will. An education which should improve this faculty would be the education par excellence."

— William James, *in a Lecture to Teachers*

In the next two chapters readers are introduced to mindfulness concepts on a continuum of time. At one end of the continuum, we have the ancient wisdom traditions that are based on thousands of years of experiential knowledge, originally passed down from one teacher to another. This is rich wisdom that calls upon our more intuitive right brain, the part of us that is willing to practice a skill rather than just conceptualize it; whether it is mindfulness, basketball, or piano playing, because it rings true in our hearts and inspires us. In this chapter we will briefly look at the wisdom traditions from which modern mindfulness springs forth.

On the other end of the continuum we will see how Western science approaches mindfulness. Coming from academic institutions, we have double-blind, peer reviewed data that proves, in a modern sense, that mindfulness practices can improve our lives on every level – from our immune systems to the way we communicate with our partners. Chapter 4 covers research data pertinent to optimum young adult development. Readers who appreciate a more linear and logical view will find this helpful.

In the middle of the continuum, the ancient wisdoms and the new scientific data converge. Here we find practical exercises that enhance the quality of modern existence. They give us a boost of confidence by showing us that we always have the ability to shape our lives for the better.

Buddhism, psychology, and mindfulness

Western contemplative practices that are found in some schools of psychology, the teachings of Buddhism, and yoga, all present models for healthy adult evolution. A basic review and understanding of these concepts will help mentors and emerging adults build motivation to experiment with the *Center Points* practices. Readers who already have a basic understanding of Buddhism, yoga, and Western psychology may find new connections in this brief overview. Suggestions for further reading have been provided in Appendix A for those readers who would like to delve further into the connections between these three interrelated schools of thought.

Exploration of the links between Buddhism, yoga, and Western psychology is not new, as we can see from William James' quote at the start of this chapter. (James was an eighteenth century educator and the first person to teach psychology in the US.) All three schools of thought seek to reduce human suffering, promote resiliency – the capacity to recover from difficulties – and self-efficacy – a healthy belief in the ability to reach goals. In addition, Buddhism, yoga, and Western psychology are all humanistic, in that they strive to focus on the whole person. They all focus on one's environment, circumstances, and behavioral reactions to the environment and circumstances. Moreover, all three schools of thought are concerned with personal moral conduct and personal values exploration as opposed to authoritative dogma. Most importantly, all three disciplines share the following:

- Exploration of thoughts and healthy behavioral responses to thoughts through present moment awareness
- Dropping into direct experience and sitting with reality in all its imperfect glory
- Increasing mature responses to circumstances that reduce suffering and increase life satisfaction for individuals and communities

Mindfulness is the intersection, the center point between Buddhism, yoga, and Western psychology.

--- ... — ... ---

Thoughts for mentors:
Pocket contemplation

As a primary care physician recently out of medical school, I try to get my patients to see the benefit of quick mindfulness practices. I was lucky to go to med school during a time when the science behind mindfulness was becoming well-known. At least half my patients are suffering from stress-related illness, and anyone with a chronic illness can benefit from these easy practices. Still, everyone is so busy these days! I'm always looking for easy, practical ways to motivate patients to try mindfulness.

As for young adults? Emerging adults can learn that dropping into the present moment for a dose of relaxation and calm can become an automatic response, just as automatic as reaching for a smartphone. It is a gift that we all possess. Much like our cell phones, however, these practices are often buried at the bottom of a bag or a pile of paperwork and can sometimes be forgotten.

I, for one, could not have survived my med school intern years without mindfulness! I'm always trying to get students to understand that taking a few seconds to be in the present moment will actually make you a more efficient student.

Direct experience, focusing in on the here-and-now, as opposed to the virtual or digital here-and-now, calms the nervous system. Don't believe me? Turn off your phone for a few minutes and take a few deep breaths. Really see the person you are eating lunch with, the view out your window, or the street on which you are walking and notice that your breathing becomes deeper and you feel more relaxed as you focus on the present moment.

Sometimes we forget that what we all have in common as human beings is a calm, peaceful core. Contemplative practices can uncover this hidden part of our experience. Mindfulness can become part of our everyday language, in the same way that smartphones have become an everyday accessory. For emerging adults this not only means better physical health, but also increased confidence, and greater satisfaction with circumstances even when those circumstances are challenging.

——————————— ... ——————————— ... ———————————

The positive psychology of Buddhism

Buddhism teaches that approximately 2,600 years ago, a sheltered Indian prince named Siddhartha left the comforts of his palace to directly experience the joy and suffering of life. It is said that when asked to summarize his teachings, Siddhartha, now known as the Buddha, said, "Take nothing as I or mine." This summary of his teachings was meant to remind his followers to keep ego and personal wants and needs in check. However, the Buddha recognized that it is human nature for the ego and external drives to be alive and well and often running the show in emerging adult lives, as well as any point in life!

The ideas of building emotion regulation and distress tolerance are fundamental to Buddhism as well as to modern Western psychology. This can be seen in The Four Noble Truths of Buddhism. These four statements gave the Buddha's followers a model by which to live every aspect of life. And just like a wise modern-day mentor, the Buddha encouraged his followers to experiment with these truths for themselves.

The Four Noble Truths

The Four Noble Truths laid out by the Buddha are:

1. It is the nature of human existence to experience suffering.
2. Suffering is brought about by our burning desire to have certain conditions, or to be free of certain conditions. These conditions are often referred to as craving and aversion.
3. There is a way out of this trap of craving and aversion.
4. The way out is the Buddhist Eightfold Path, which presents a system of living that will increase peacefulness and reduce suffering.

The first noble truth states that we cannot escape suffering. The Buddha taught that as human beings we are vulnerable to not only hunger and pain, but also psychological suffering such as fear, loneliness, and hatred. If we were lucky enough to leave childhood and adolescence without suffering, we are almost assuredly going to get a taste of it in emerging adulthood. This is not meant to be a gloomy prediction. On the contrary, the Buddha was trying to

71

show his followers that craving and aversion, joy and suffering are just part of the human condition, and if we can embrace this fact we might realize that we are all connected. Some frequent categories of suffering I see with the emerging adults in my counseling practice include trouble finding meaningful employment, achieving financial stability, successfully navigating the world of dating, and the pain of seeing changes in social groups.

The second noble truth summarizes the causes of suffering as craving and aversion. Here the Buddha taught that all suffering arises from our desire to control our environment either by pushing away from objects, situations, and people that displease us or pulling toward objects, situations, and people we desire. Luckily, the third noble truth gives us hope in the fact that just as naturally as suffering arises, it also falls away, and we can help this falling away process to happen by practicing the fourth noble truth, which is known as the Eightfold Path.

The Eightfold Path

This Path is essentially a prescription for attaining what Buddhists refer to as enlightenment, and what many Eastern and Western practitioners would consider spiritual maturity. Some level of spiritual maturity, or put in more secular terms, optimum maturity, is what we are after when introducing mindfulness as a practical skill for healthy adult development.

We will limit our discussion of the Eightfold Path to how it can be applied to helping healthy emerging adult development, and what positive psychologists would call the good life – a life that highlights one's personal strengths, provides pleasant and meaningful experiences, and offers service to others. It is on this Eightfold Path that we are presented with support for mindfulness meditation. It is in the Eightfold Path that we will see similar paradigms to the basic tenets of Western psychology and classical yogic philosophy. Let's take a quick look at these eight steps in terms of healthy development in emerging adulthood. Keep the above definition of a *good life* in mind as you read:

1. Right View – the word right is used at several steps along the Eightfold Path. We can easily replace the word right with wholesome or whole. Right view does not judge a point of view as right or wrong, but encourages a view that is life affirming and conducive to growth.

2. Right Intention – sometimes right intention is referred to as right thought or right resolve. Building the idea of right intention in emerging adults is a wonderful gift that can help create a virtuous cycle of healthy decision-making.

3. Right Speech – right speech includes refraining from lying, gossiping, or speaking rudely to others. This step of the path, like all the others will take a lifetime of practice. In the twenty-first century right speech may translate into fewer social media faux pas, and better communication in new relationships or jobs.

4. Right Action – right action refers to taking action that reduces suffering. If emerging adults have a basic awareness and understanding of the pitfalls of over-attachment to ego needs and craving, they are more likely to make decisions that have a long-term net benefit towards themselves and others. In Tracey's case, the goal was to get her to think more mindfully about her personal vision of career and relationship as opposed to her parents' goals. Meditating on right action will help her start to build her own authentic vision of right action.

5. Right Livelihood – right livelihood refers to work that does not cheat or harm others. It also refers to our attitude toward work. This idea of focusing on our work itself and letting go of the fruit of our work is also a major theme in yoga and is the focus of the *Bhagavad Gita,* the famous Hindu scripture about karma yoga or the yoga of action.

If, in young adulthood, we can examine the idea of making holistic career choices, not so much driven by external ego-needs, but by what is sustainable, what we deeply value and find meaningful, we are likely to experience more contentment, and most likely experience more success.

6. Right Effort – when we are focusing on the present moment, being mindful, we experience more ease and there is a natural release of straining, forcing, or pulling. Western psychology sometimes refers to this ease of effort as flow: That state of optimum absorption in an activity where we feel productive and peaceful.

7. Right Mindfulness – right mindfulness asks the practitioner to pay attention to the states of mind that cause suffering. By watching our thoughts and the states that bring about suffering, we are practicing right mindfulness. By separating our thoughts from actions on a regular basis with a small but steady mindfulness practice, emerging adult practitioners like Darcy and Jake will start to make decisions that lead to less suffering, more confidence and satisfaction, and reduce the prevalence of the cycle of craving and aversion.

8.   Right Meditation – right meditation is the formal practice of training the mind so that it becomes focused, centered, and aware. It is this actual formal meditation practice that helps bring about right effort or right mindfulness.

Developmental psychology points to emerging adulthood as a major transition time. Typically during this transition time, much like adolescence, the dawn of middle adulthood, and other key life transitions, we are faced with a motherlode of cravings and aversions. In emerging adulthood we strive for the anchors of financial security and intimacy, and recoil from certain identities that we find displeasing. In extreme cases, emerging adulthood is the time when we are angrily casting off any remnants of childhood or cultural expectations. Conversely we may be clinging desperately to a dependent state in an attempt to feel safe. These are examples of difficulty with integrating and passing through Erikson's stages, difficulties that match up with the Buddhist idea of suffering caused by craving and aversion. It's a time where we might have a burning desire that we will stop at nothing to attain, or a time when we feel overwhelmed, railing against the process of setting up our own independent lives.

--- ... — ... ---

Thoughts for mentors:
Contemplate a burning desire

Think of a time in your emerging adult years when you had a burning desire that seemed all encompassing. For this exercise, it doesn't matter if the goal was healthy or unhealthy, helpful or harmful to your development and to those you came in contact with. For now, try to think back to that goal and remember your motivation. Did it involve belonging to a certain group? Obtaining a particular financial or career goal? Maybe it was to stay carefree, unencumbered by any serious relationship or career responsibility. Connecting with that burning desire of the past, can you see how this craving may have caused you some discomfort? Can you remember a moment when you had some clarity about your motivation that perhaps helped you fine-tune your goal, creating more flexibility and contentment around it? Perhaps an "aha" moment that helped you cling less desperately to that burning desire and helped you in creating a sense that you were, essentially, already okay? Can you identify the activities or conditions that helped you find this clarity and help you reduce any uncomfortable craving or aversion attached to the goal?

75

Chances are activities that gave you clarity were contemplative-based: A walk in nature, time talking with a good friend or trusted mentor, or quiet time alone. Maybe a religious practice from your family of origin helped you find balance, or something as simple as a long bike ride, listening to or playing music. Recall times of contemplation that helped you reach, or maybe saved you, from a burning desire. How would you talk about this experience with an emerging adult in your life?

_____ ⋯ _____ ⋯ _____

_____ ⋯ — ⋯ _____

Voices of Emerging Adults:
Tracey waking up

I can't believe I broke down crying in my counseling session today. I've been going for eight weeks now. What is my problem! I guess it's because I'm realizing that I've been doing what other people expect of me my whole damn life.

As for marrying Peter, I feel like he is more of a business partner than a fiancé, but my family loves him. I do really love him too… I think. I don't really know what the hell that means. My parents are divorced. I definitely don't want to go down that road. Donna asked me if I could think of a committed couple that I could use as a model of a healthy relationship. I told her that, even though my mom and step-dad argue sometimes, I can see they really care about each other, and they seem to really respect and appreciate each other. I've seen them both calm each other down at stressful times too.

She also asked me to think about what it means to be independent. This was helpful because I realized that being independent doesn't necessarily mean being alone. On the other hand being in a relationship will not solve all my anxiety.

I love the homework assignment we came up with. The goal is for me to sit with some of the discomfort I feel about being alone. I'm going to set up an at-home mini-mindfulness retreat this weekend. My roommate is going to be away so it's the perfect time for me to give it a try.

I'm supposed to keep away from Facebook, and Netflix, and other online distractions, and instead work on some art or journaling if I feel bored. I'm also supposed to do at least three mini-meditations or gentle yoga sessions, and back off on my seven-mile runs, at least for this weekend. I'll track my moods and thoughts three times a day too. Donna suggested I use a couple of prompt questions when I'm tracking my mood, like, "What do I most need right now to feel peaceful?" and "What is my heart's deepest longing?" I'm actually looking forward to a quiet weekend!

Another model for healthy emerging adult development found in Buddhist teachings is particularly important in helping emerging adults manage the ups and downs of early adult life. This model is known as the Four Immeasurables.

In Buddhism there exist four emotional states that are revered as elixirs to human suffering. The term Four Immeasurables is derived from their limitless power to transform suffering. When practiced they have the ability to open us up to the present moment, tame our personal agendas, and regulate our thoughts, emotions, and behaviors.

1. **Equanimity** builds one's ability to be less reactive. It can help emerging adults build the skills to stay even-minded in the midst of daily gain and loss, and therefore maintain physical balance and mental focus. It is said to be the antidote to prejudice and harsh judgment.
2. **Loving-kindness,** defined as the genuine, friendly and kind-hearted concern for the well-being of others (and oneself) can help emerging adults build a strong sense of belonging. It is said to be the antidote to anger.
3. **Compassion,** a heartfelt yearning to see all beings (including oneself) be free of suffering which ultimately leads to greater meaning and sense of connection to the human race. It is said to be the antidote to fear.
4. **Empathetic joy,** which is an uninhibited delight in one's own and others' joy and good fortune. Empathetic joy can act as an antidote to the modern curse of over-comparison that so many emerging adults struggle with now that we have daily access to our peers' every activity thanks to social media. It is said to be the antidote to jealousy.

Yogic philosophers also acknowledge the Four Immeasurables. Although their names are different, The Divine Abodes – Upekka, Maitri, Karuna, Mudita, signify respectively, the ideas of equanimity, loving-kindness, compassion, and empathetic joy. We can see how these four ideas can help heal developmental trauma, and help young adults like Darcy get back on track.

Finding refuge

Buddhism, yoga, and Western psychology all stress the importance of finding a like-minded group, and taking refuge – finding comfort – in a group of individuals who respect and share our values.

Voices of Emerging Adults
Darcy - Finding refuge with a like-minded group

Before I left for school my favorite cousin gave me the advice to surround myself with good people. Of course I shrugged this off. I always found good people to be kind of shallow and boring. But what am I getting out of choosing friends by how they dress, or by which parties they go to? In my freshman year there was this really nice guy in my dorm. He was cute too and I could tell he was interested in me. I just ignored him though. I don't know why. Looking back on it now, I think I might have been freaked out by how nice he was being to me. I just didn't even know what to do with that. I talked to Donna about this screwed up pattern I have of being interested in people who clearly don't really care about me or seem mysterious in some way. She suggested I take my cousin's advice and put a spin on it – to surround myself with like-minded people – people who share similar values – like treating people with compassion. The advice goes well with my work on increasing self-compassion too. The first session of the mindfulness for grad students group was much more interesting than I thought it would be. When I went last week I heard a few stories that made me feel less awkward. It was good to hear that I'm not alone in my struggles to practice self-care, and to hear how people make mindfulness work in their lives. Maybe I'll find some good people in this group.

Yoga and mindfulness

Darcy is having some success with simple loving-kindness practices and adopting the idea of self-compassion. However, sitting still in meditation is not always the best prescription for anxious or depressed emerging adults. Sometimes physical movement is needed. This is where yoga comes in as the appropriate contemplative exercise. Yoga, like Buddhism, asks the practitioner to come back to direct experience through systematically observing the mind and body. It is a moving meditation, and can be much more effective for healing developmental trauma, especially for emerging adults who are accustomed to a lot of physical activity.

The word yoga itself literally means to unite, referring to the union of body and mind. Like Buddhism, it is an ancient practice that can be traced back over thousands of years. The description of yoga used here relies on what is considered classical or Ashtanga yoga. Classical yoga is a methodology of holistic self-development outlined by the sage Patanjali circa 200 CE, the author of the Yoga Sutras, a text that describes the Eight Limbs of yoga. There are many similarities between the Buddha's Eightfold Path and Patanjali's Eight Limbs. (In fact the story of Buddha's enlightenment includes time spent with ascetic yogis.) Both place similar importance on the process of quieting the mind, practicing emotion regulation, and cultivating wise action through contemplative practices like mindfulness.

The Eight Limbs of Patanjali's yoga are listed below. As you read through, notice the similarities between the Eight Limbs and the Buddha's Eightfold Path. Also notice the focus on mindfulness.

1. The Yamas – describe social restraints. The Five Yamas are nonviolence (Ahimsa in Sanskrit), truthfulness (Satya), non-stealing (Asteya), moderation (Bramacharya), and non-attachment (Aparigraha) to people or objects.

80

2. Niyamas – are observances or disciplines to be cultivated. The Five Niyamas are purity (Saucha), contentment (Santosha), austerity (Tapas), self-inquiry (Svadhyaya), and surrender to the divine (Ishvara-Pranidhana). Together the Yamas and the Niyamas make up a set of ethical guidelines for yogis.

3. Asana – Asanas are the actual physical postures that have become so popular in the West. Because of their popularity there is a growing body of scientific evidence to back up their ability to foster physical and mental well-being.

4. Pranayama – refers to breath control. Together Asana and Pranayama make up the typical yoga class of the Western world. Because of the rise in popularity of yoga in our culture, these two limbs will be familiar to most emerging adults. Most college campuses and for that matter, town and city centers, offer a variety of yoga styles from which to choose. Just focusing on Asana and Pranayama can be life changing, but it is interesting to note that the first four limbs of yoga are meant to steady the mind and body for mindfulness and meditation.

5. Pratyahara – refers to withdrawal of attention from the senses. Here the yogi moves inward. As mentioned above, the first four limbs are said to purify the body, allowing the yoga practitioner to turn his or her attention toward the spiritual realm by building discipline over sensory distractions. Pratyahara encourages practitioners to take a break from sensory overload – a welcome respite in the digital age.

6. Dharana – is defined as concentration or one-pointedness. Together Pratyahara and Dharana can be likened to the Buddhist concept of right mindfulness in that the yogi is asked to begin cultivating instances of present-moment absorption. Patanjali was way ahead of his time by encouraging these practices. We now know that this present moment absorption changes the brain in such a way that allows for better communication, decision-making, better control of the stress response, and a stronger feeling of connectedness with community – qualities that can greatly improve the lives of emerging adults in transition.

7. Dhyana – meditation this is the formal practice of one-pointed concentration, similar to right meditation in the Buddhist Eightfold path.

8. Samadhi – or Nirvana is a state of self-realization, much like the idea of enlightenment in Buddhism. Yogis sometimes describe this as a state of oneness with the divine. Like the Buddhist state of Nirvana, we can think of Samadhi as a certain level of super-maturity that, we may or may not attain. Enlightenment or Nirvana is not the practical goal when using these systems. Remember, in *Mindfulness for Emerging Adults* we are seeking the practical goal of a good life through balance, belonging, focus, and meaning, with super or optimal maturity remaining a lifelong journey.

In his book *Yoga and the Quest for True Self,* Stephen Cope points out that yoga is a practice of moving inward, a journey away from the material world and our over-identification with it, allowing the practitioner to find his or her way back to the true self (1999).

--- ··· — ··· ---

Thoughts for mentors:
A yoga teacher's thoughts on distraction

When I first started teaching yoga and learning about the yoga philosophy laid out by Patanjali, I wondered what practitioners of Patanjali's time found to be so distracting. After all, dinging cells phones or neon billboards did not interrupt them. But the fact that even 5,000 years ago humans were looking for a way to quiet the mind, and balance the ups and downs of daily life tells you just how hardwired the human nervous system is to be on the lookout for danger. Our senses are the door to many pleasures as well as many pains, especially in emerging adulthood. The younger adults who come to my classes often tell me that they will sit down to take care of important work on their laptops, and suddenly find themselves monitoring acquaintances' activities on Facebook. I have to admit, even at age 40, now that I'm using Facebook and other social media to get the word out about my classes, I find myself falling into the Facebook trap. Small doses of tuning out digital as well as other forms of distractions can feel like a sanctuary these days.

--- ··· --- ··· ---

Western psychology and mindfulness

Eastern thought has made a slow and increasing impact on Western psychology and, in fact, Western culture as a whole. This can be seen in the development of the humanistic branch of psychology as well as more modern schools. Humanistic theory states that humans have an innate drive to be compassionate and contribute to society in a positive way. Several psychoanalytic pioneers, like Erich Fromm and Karen Horney, both took an interest in Buddhism later in their careers. Presently Buddhist concepts are being used in Dialectical Behavioral Therapy (DBT), a treatment developed by Marsha Linehan for patients suffering from Borderline Personality Disorder (BPD), a disorder characterized by poor emotional regulation and volatile personal relationships.

Another widely accepted therapy, Mindfulness-Based Cognitive Therapy (MBCT), builds awareness of thought patterns, emotional reactions to these patterns and their effect on the mind and body through various contemplative exercises.

Authenticity as a common goal

Several main concepts bridge the worlds of Buddhism, yoga, and Western psychology. One such bridge is the idea of the false self. D. W. Winnicott, one of the fathers of attachment theory, the study of how our bond with primary caregivers shapes future attachments, believed that the false self is born when we are not fully accepted by our caregivers. He theorized that, when placed with a caregiver who is not able to give us unconditional love, usually because of their own unfinished development, we give up our genuine selves to become the child the caregiver needs us to be. It is under these conditions that the false self is born, and we lose our connection to our true selves.

—————————————— ··· — ··· ——————————————

Thoughts for mentors:
How is your heart?

My 25 year-old niece, Jenna, is one of my favorite people in the world! She's smart and super funny. She always cuts through the tension at family gatherings. And yet, sometimes I find myself slipping into the annoying old aunt role by asking the questions that all young adults hate to hear, such as, "How's the job search going?" and "What are your plans for the summer?" It's like I can't help myself. At least I can draw the line at, "Are you dating anyone?"

I think we older adults start in with this line of questioning because we are trying to connect with the younger ones. But inevitably, it backfires. It's not always easy and it doesn't always work, but I've been trying to ask more meaningful questions like, "How's your new apartment? Are you still able to connect with your friends from high school?" Questions like these, topics that make Jenna feel really cared about, have led to better conversations. She seems to trust me more when I ask her questions about social connection. She has opened up to me and has told me about living alone. We've been able to have some good conversations about managing loneliness and trying to be independent. I think she feels understood. It's a more satisfying conversation for both of us.

——————————— ⋯ ——————————— ⋯ ———————————

Learning to be authentic is a powerful skill that can help with self-regulation and self-confidence. Unfortunately, many emerging adults struggle with identifying their authentic selves, especially after years of following parental and educational mandates, and chasing societal expectations. It is the journey back to the genuine self, this longing to feel at home in our bodies in the present moment, that is the fundamental concept emerging from both Eastern philosophies and Western psychotherapy, and the foundation of the *Center Points* exercises.

Emotion regulation as another common goal

In his book, *Wake Up To Your Life* (2002), Buddhist teacher Ken McLeod notes the human tendency to label emotions as good or bad. He notes that in contrast, Buddhism focuses on reaction and response to emotion. This small but powerful shift in focus from labeling emotions as good or bad, to a focus on reaction and response to situations is key to healthy and optimum human development, and can create healthier personal life choices for emerging adults.

―――――――――――――――― ... — ... ――――――――――――――――

Voices of Emerging Adults:
Tracey Emerges from her mini-retreat

In my next session with Tracey she arrived with her homework completed and with some fresh insight after having a taste of what it feels like to tend to the true self. She gave the following account of her experience during her at-home retreat:

The mini-retreat weekend was quite interesting. At first I was restless and had trouble settling in, so I spent Friday night organizing for my quiet weekend. I did my first mindfulness break at around 9pm on Friday night, using an app that I downloaded to my phone. I remember feeling a little sad, but remembered my instructions to just sit with the emotions for a little bit before looking for a distraction. The next thing I knew it was 7am on Saturday morning – I just passed out! I guess I didn't realize how tired I was! I don't usually get up that early on the weekends, but I got up and went for a walk by the river, instead of my usual run. It was a little difficult not to start running, especially when so many people my age were flying by me.

When I got home I did my second mindfulness session. I didn't fall asleep this time but I was wishing I could! That sad, uneasy feeling came up again and I was starting to feel panicky. I started thinking about checking my email, but I had made an agreement with myself not to do that until noon. I stuck with my breath and noticed that being a little lonely and sad wasn't killing me. In fact it was preferable to the panic, and I was feeling pretty good about not reacting to a little sadness in the same old way that's keeping me trapped in fear about my future.

Over the course of the day on Saturday I did about four or five more mini-mindfulness sessions and after each I worked on journaling about the questions Donna gave me. I focused on the one about what I needed to be more peaceful. I still felt restless, but I didn't freak out. I decided that I really don't like my job as much as I was pretending to. I feel like an impostor there most of the time. When I was little I wanted to be an illustrator and write children's books. I was always thinking up stories and drawing characters to go along with them. I also realized I do really care about Peter. I want to figure out a way to get to know him better, though. I'm realizing I have a lot of work to do and a lot of hard decisions to make.

Usually when I realize I have a lot of work to do I get really anxious. I couldn't believe how calm I was Saturday night and Sunday morning. By Sunday afternoon though, after looking at my calendar for Monday I started getting stressed again. The at-home retreat was nice and relaxing and everything, and I'm glad I'm being more honest with myself about my doubts about getting married, but I'm not sure what to do next.

———————————— ... ———————————— ... ————————————

What happens when you stop?

Tracey is experiencing a pretty normal reaction to suddenly dropping into mindfulness after years in "doing" mode. A group of therapists I worked with used to joke around by saying "this mindfulness is killing us," referring to the discomfort that can arise when we first try to put the breaks on habitual busyness. It can feel really difficult, especially for goal-driven emerging adults, to stop and take a taste of direct experience. And like Tracey, many high-functioning people who first try mindfulness are doubtful about the practical application of such a skill. However, neuroscience research is revealing contemplative practices are indeed practical, showing increased activity in the areas of the brain that help us communicate better, control reactions to stress, and more easily express creativity – all important skills in the workplace. In Chapter 4, we will look at some of the latest research on mindfulness and similar contemplative practices to see how we might help emerging adults like Tracey trust in the idea of slowing down to get ahead, both professionally and personally.

Summary

Since the very beginnings of the rise of Western psychology, scholars have made connections between psychological theory, Buddhism, and other Eastern Philosophies. These schools of thought, that all share mindfulness and other contemplative practices as a center point, provide an opportunity for adults to develop their own unique set of values, develop authentic identity, and have an easier relationship with the present moment, even in our current culture of accelerated change.

CHAPTER 4

The Science
Developing motivation to make mindfulness a habit

Traditional knowledge brings together the seen and the unseen, whereas Western science says that if we can't measure something, it doesn't exist.

— Robin Wall Kimmerer

Mindfulness research specific to young adult development

Over the last forty years clinical research on mindfulness and related interventions has exploded. Articles about mindfulness can be found in mainstream media like the *New York Times* and *The Huffington Post*, as well as highly regarded peer-reviewed professional journals. Some people feel that these peer-reviewed studies give credence to what Eastern sages have know for centuries – that contemplative practice like mindfulness and yoga can reduce stress and increase life satisfaction.

The deluge of mindfulness research can be overwhelming to sift through. This chapter presents a brief overview of the research. Wherever possible, I chose studies that focused on emerging adults. As Botanist Robin Wall Kimmerer stated in an interview in *The Sun Magazine*, traditional knowledge like that found in the Yoga Sutras brings together the seen and unseen. While many people will be inspired by the rich philosophical and spiritual traditions from which mindfulness springs, others will be inspired by the scientific research conducted on mindfulness-informed practices. What will motivate you to make room for mindfulness in your busy life, the ancient history, or modern science?

The rising popularity of mindfulness in the West, along with advances in neuroimaging, has also brought about new fields of study. Psychoneuroimmunology (the study of the link between the brain and the immune system), psychoneuroendocrinology (the study of hormone fluctuation and human behavior), and interpersonal neurobiology (the study of how relationships foster or inhibit healthy brain development) are now important areas of research that explore the efficacy of using contemplative practices like mindfulness as a means to maximize mental and physical health. Prestigious academic centers like Brown University now have developed Contemplative Studies programs, which serve as interdisciplinary think tanks for exploring the connection between behavior and the positive social impact of contemplative practices.

Even with all the evidence at our fingertips, sitting quietly, meditating, even practicing gentle yoga may not be priorities for energetic young adults. However, making and keeping social connections and feeling a sense of mastery of daily life tasks are indeed high priorities for emerging adults. Several studies using emerging adults show that mindfulness can be used as a life skill that will foster success in relationships, in academic settings, and on the job. Let's examine data from recent studies that look at the connection between mindfulness practices, and the successful ability to balance the nervous system, to improve communication, interpersonal connection, emotion regulation, physical health, and attention – all important aspects of successful emerging adult development.

The Research

Emotion Regulation: Emerging adults with a strong ability to regulate their emotions in social situations will have an easier time navigating the major domains of work and love. The emerging adult who can read his supervisor's mood, or stay calm in the midst of romantic disappointment is practicing mindfulness and emotion regulation in a very adaptive way. A study published in the *Journal of Cognition and Emotion* in 2013 showed that mindfulness skills can increase emotion regulation in an emerging adult sample. Researchers took pairs of emerging adults, "romantic couples" in fact, and put them through a battery of psychological tests including the Mindful Attention and Awareness Scale (MAAS), and the Emotions Regulation Scale. Participants were also asked to take the Emotion Go/No Go test, a well-known testing instrument that measures behavioral inhibition, by looking at participants' ability to accurately recognize and label facial expressions. Participants were then asked to download a smartphone application that would "ping" them, and enable them to report their perception of social experiences in real time over the next six days.

The researchers found that higher levels of mindfulness as found by the MAAS correlated with success with the Emotion Go/No go test, and predicted greater present-moment well-being, as well as a more positive mood at time of report. The high-mindfulness group also reported greater emotional stability.

Think back to Jake who is having such difficulty managing his emotions that he was resorting to self-destructive behavior. The above study shows that if Jake is willing to keep practicing the mindfulness techniques we discussed like deep breathing, watching stress levels and thought patterns throughout the day, and spending time in nature, he can improve levels of emotion regulation.

91

Linking mindfulness practices to current life challenges

A randomized controlled study conducted at Duke University in 2012/2013 based on the Koru program, a mindfulness training program offered to emerging adults on college campuses and in the workplace, resulted in participants experiencing a greater sense of calm, feeling more rested, and higher levels of self-compassion. The results were replicated in the wait-list group. The Koru program is specifically designed for college students and builds motivation for participation by concentrating on emerging adult developmental strivings. Participants meet in small peer groups where social connections can be made. Practice sessions are short and mindfulness exercises are linked to academic and work scenarios. The Koru program continues to gain popularity in college and work settings.

Being able to put the breaks on harsh judgments of self and others is an important life skill that will help anyone in transition to feel more comfortable in their own skin. It will also help them build close relationships. Exploring this important work with a group of peers can be a life-changing experience. In Buddhism there is a strong tradition of relying on a group of like-minded individuals. Darcy got a taste of how powerful this can be by attending a meditation group. By being around other grad students who were also working to find balance, belonging, focus and meaning through group meditation and discussion, Darcy was not only able to put mindfulness-informed practices to work in her life, but also forged new social connections.

Being less judgmental of one's experience leads to greater emotional health. Another recent study published in 2014 in *Personality in Individual Differences* used a research instrument called the Five Facet Mindfulness Questionnaire to distinguish between different components of mindful awareness and the emotional health of a group of college students who did not have prior experience with meditating. Those subjects scoring high on an index as high-mindfulness and non-judgmentally aware were able to use adaptive emotional outcomes more effectively, compared to low-mindfulness groups and judgmentally observing groups. The latter scored higher in depressive symptoms, anxiety, affect instability, and distress intolerance. This study suggests that being able to observe and refrain from harsh thoughts, and exhibiting compassion and self-compassion can prevent depressive mood and low resiliency. There is mounting scientific evidence that shows us that self-compassion improves performance in work and love, yet many emerging adults remain suspicious of the idea of extending compassion inward. We could see this with Tracey who was afraid that mindfulness-informed stress reduction practices would make her somehow less ambitious.

In 2009, I attended a series of lectures sponsored by Yongey Mingyur Rinpoche, a Tibetan Buddhist monk who has become quite popular in the United States, partially due to his candid style of relating his own struggles with anxiety as a child in Nepal. At one lecture, Yongey Mingyur Rinpoche stated, "Mindfulness can help you do more with less effort." My first thought was that his comment sounded like a sales slogan for mindfulness. But my own experience with mindfulness practices and the research proves his statement to be true – we are able to take care of our duties, make better decisions, and be more creative with mindfulness practices. Tracey not only can stay competitive at work, but she can do so with more ease.

Decreasing anxiety, increasing empathy in professional settings

Social intelligence and the ability to express appropriate compassion and empathy have been shown to be an important component of successful patient-doctor relationships. Yet physicians report burnout (and an associated decline in empathy) at a higher rate than individuals in other professions, according to a 2012 study published in the Journals – American Medical Association

93

(JAMA). Dozens of medical schools including Tufts Medical Center, Brown University, and the Rush University Medical Center in Chicago are now offering classes on mindfulness-based practices as part of physician training. Much like Kristin Neff's work on self-compassion, the JAMA study shows the benefits of balancing self-care with compassionate care for others to maintain job satisfaction and decrease physician burnout.

Research on yoga and other forms of mindful movement

It is said that the Buddha taught thousands of different ways to meditate to get his teachings across to as many people as possible. For highly anxious emerging adults, like Jake, sitting meditation may be counter-productive. This is why I suggest talking to emerging adults about different forms of mindful movement as well as traditional meditation. Research on yoga and other forms of mindful movement is slowly starting to catch up with the research on mindfulness. In spite of its popularity in the West, funding for research on yoga and related contemplative practices continues to be dwarfed by funding for studies looking at psychoactive medication and other mainstream forms of mental health treatment. Nevertheless it is gaining momentum.

The Waisman Center at the University of Wisconsin has published many well-regarded studies showing the impact of contemplative practices on the mind and brain. One such study completed in 2014 looked at the benefits of Tai Chi training including improving attention in healthy emerging adults. The study used self-reports backed by neurological measurements. Outcomes showed that this slow meditative movement provided participants with a stronger ability to focus, and decreased impulsivity. This research gives preliminary support for using Tai Chi as an adjunct, possibly even as an alternative to mainstream treatment for attention deficit.

Increase activity in areas of the brain associated with positive mood

Yoga therapy research continues to mount, thanks in part to the interest in using yoga as a treatment for military personnel returning from Iraq and Afghanistan, many of whom are emerging adults. In her books, *Yoga for Depression (2003),* and *Yoga Skills for Therapists (2012),* Amy Weintraub points to yoga's ability to calm the nervous system, causing a cascade of biological changes, including an increase in GABA production in the brain. GABA is a neurotransmitter implicated in calming the nervous system as it puts the breaks on the fight or flight response. Practicing yoga has also been shown to decrease cortisol levels, and increase BDNF, brain-derived neurotropic factor, which facilitates neuronal communication, helping practitioners integrate and learn from experience.

In addition yoga helps tone the nervous system, making it more adaptable to stress. Yoga and meditation have also been shown to increase levels of melatonin, helping to regulate circadian rhythms, sleep, and mood. Most studies involving yoga, meditation and the like, required participants to commit to regular practice for six to eight weeks, but results can be seen in brain imaging after just twenty minutes of exercise!

--- ⋯ — ⋯ ---

Voices of Emerging Adults
Isabel thinks on her feet

I was all set to sign a lease on an apartment with my high school friend last week, even though part of me knew I was rushing things. I got some cash for my birthday, which is great, but I wasn't sure how many shifts I was going to be able to pick up at my old job. I was going to go for it anyway. Donna suggested that I go for a long mindful walk to think about this one decision. My instructions were to walk around the pond at the reservoir two times. The first time I was supposed to turn off my brain and keep returning to my breath. I didn't do it perfectly, but by the end of the first loop, which took about twenty minutes, I felt calmer. The second time around I was supposed to think about what was driving my decision. I realized that I was being impatient, and was letting thoughts like, "only losers live with their parents" drive my decision. I decided to wait one more month. It felt really good to not let my emotions control my behavior for once!

—— ··· ——————— ··· ————

Balancing energy and the stress response

Another yoga study published in *Alternative Therapies in Health and Medicine* (2004), directly relates to emerging adults and emotion regulation. This study took 28 participants between the ages of 18 and 28, all of whom were experiencing mild symptoms of depression. Participants attended two, one-hour Iyengar style yoga classes per week for a period of five weeks. B. K. S. Iyengar's impact on modern yoga in the West can not be overstated. The Iyengar style is known for focus on proper alignment, using props to help individual adjust to their level of ability. Iyengar also identifies the mood-balancing, psychological qualities to certain yoga poses.

This study focused on back bends, inversions and standing poses that are believed to relieve depression and regulate energy, according to the Iyengar School. Participants reported significant decreases of depression and associated anxiety. The decreases became noticeable in the middle of the five-week intervention. Participants also reported increased energy at the end of each class as well as decreased levels of negative mood.

Ease of being – no matter what

An overall trend emerges from studies using mindfulness-based interventions. Researchers following cancer patients, care-givers of family members with dementia, and those suffering from chronic pain show that what changes most after starting a meditation or yoga practice is not one's circumstances, but ones relationship to the circumstances. After participating in these interventions, study after study shows an increased sense of self-efficacy. For example:

- I can do this with acceptance.
- I can make meaning and learn from this.
- I'm not alone in this.
- I'm doing the best I can.
- What matters is my ability to be caring.
- I can find peace with this task showing increased levels of compassion and empathy for self and others.

You can see this same result with Isabel, Darcy, Jake, and Tracey. Their circumstances did not change drastically as a result of practicing contemplative exercises, but acceptance and self-compassion are helping them to let go of unhelpful thought and behavior patterns and make wise decisions. And even though they would all like their life circumstances to be a little different, acceptance and self-compassion are balancing their nervous systems and helping them act with clarity, calm, and confidence. Over time, these practices will help them feel more in control and feel more life-satisfaction.

From state to trait – changes in the physical structure of the brain

A functional MRI (fMRI) shows which area of the brain is working as a result of a certain activity, based on the blood flow. This technology allows researchers to look at the changes in the brain that come about as result of activity or change in mood state, even capturing the changes in the brain of the mindfulness practitioner. Scientists have been able to show that increased levels of activation in the left prefrontal region of the brain are associated with the experience and expression of positive affect and emotion. Conversely, increased levels of right prefrontal activation are associated with increased expression of negative emotion and affect. Studies looking at mindfulness-based interventions repeatedly show increases in left-brain activity post-intervention.

Research recently conducted by Sara Lazar at Massachusetts General Hospital (2011), showed increased thickness of cerebral cortex in mindfulness meditators compared to the brains of control subjects. These studies show us that mindfulness not only creates states of calm, clarity and connectedness, but that over time these mood states and associated behavior can become traits – physically and behaviorally a more permanent part of who we are. These reports show that the effects of meditation go beyond the meditation session itself, much in the same way that exercise improves muscle tone after a physical exercise routine has been completed.

Overall, mindfulness practices have been shown to move frontal lobe activity from the right prefrontal area of the brain toward the left prefrontal area. Dr. Kelly McGonigal, a researcher at Stanford University, describes this shift as moving from the self-referential mind that is responsible for social comparison and ruminating on past and future events, to the experiential mind that governs the ability to focus on the present moment and approach experiences with less anxiety (2012). For better or worse the self-referential brain is our default human condition. The benefit of the default mode is that it allows us to plan, remember, and avoid danger. The drawback of this default mode is that it often finds danger where there really is none. Left prefrontal activity, the gift of contemplative practices, provides access to increased emotion regulation and bodily control, greater ability to modulate anxiety and depression, increased tolerance to pain, greater self-awareness, as well as the ability to set goals and increased empathy.

··· — ···

Thoughts for mentors:
A yoga teacher builds motivation

Just as physical exercise helps us build muscle, increase coordination, and improve heart health, meditation helps activate areas of the brain that help us feel more pleasantly engaged with the world. That's the good news, but the truth is, just like exercise, we can't just do one workout a year and expect to see results.

Even yoga teachers sometimes struggle with keeping up with mindfulness practices. I find giving scientific tidbits to my students (and to myself) can really keep me motivated to practice. I think especially the younger adults in my class need to be reminded that contemplative exercises are not just a nice idea, but a tool that can improve social interaction, decision-making, and help find happiness.

Here's a summary of facts that I often refer to in my classes:
- Meditation increases activity in the brain regions used for paying attention and making decisions.
- Studies show that individuals who take part in meditation programs have more activity in the left pre-frontal cortex – the area of the brain associated with positive emotions.
- Yoga helps tone the parasympathetic nervous system – the rest and digest portion of our nervous system, and tame the fight or flight response, helping you to maintain calm in social situations.

- Researchers at Harvard Medical School have shown increases in GABA, (an inhibitory neurotransmitter) in meditators. Low levels of GABA are associated with depression and anxiety disorders, so more GABA is good.
- Mindfulness and yoga increase interoceptive awareness, or the sense of what is going on in ones own body.
- Different breathing techniques used in stress reduction training can help increase or calm energy. Young adults can learn breathing techniques that will help them feel more alert at work or school, or feel more calm and relaxed in social settings.
- Yoga and meditation have been shown to increase melatonin, helping to regulate circadian rhythms, sleep, and mood.
- Yoga has been shown to reduce cortisol, a key hormone in the stress response. Cortisol increases blood pressure, blood sugar, and suppresses the immune system.
- Yoga and meditation increase alpha brain waves. Alpha brain waves are associated with relaxation and creativity.
- Yoga and meditation facilitate neuroplasticity, the brains ability to change structurally in response to experience.
- Through yoga, meditation, and mindfulness-based cognitive therapy exercises, individuals can moderate bad habits and tame obsessive thoughts and compulsive behaviors.
- Memorize Hebb's axiom: "Neurons that fire together, wire together". This phrase summarizes the fact that brain processes that are exercised build strong networks over time.

——————————— ⋯ ——————————— ⋯ ———————————

Summary

Mindfulness is an excellent complementary treatment for a variety of health and wellness concerns and aligns with scientifically-backed theories in modern psychology. Both disciplines focus on increasing resiliency in the face of the inevitable difficulties that we experience in adulthood, as well as increasing the frequency of experiencing contentment and joy. Although these mindfulness-informed practices don't magically change life circumstances, they can help emerging adults cope with rapid change and life transitions as well as enable us to more fully savor success.

PART III

How to Build a Personalized Toolbox of Contemplative Practice

Thus far, the strong connection between Eastern and Western contemplative traditions and healthy emerging adult development has been explored. By listening to the voices of Isabel, Jake, Darcy and Tracey, we learned that each journey through young adulthood is unique. It's a time of life when we may be working to integrate many different stages of psychosocial development. We see Isabel is trying to stay balanced and centered in the present moment and to use technology to enhance life instead of to hide from her aspirations. Darcy is learning to practice self-compassion and maintain healthy boundaries, and attempting to circle back and heal the relational trauma she experienced as a young teenager. Jake is learning how to take care of his basic needs without relying too heavily on his partner. He is also trying to quiet his mind so that he can make good decisions. Tracey is learning how to slow down and follow her own dreams as opposed to blindly following the dreams prescribed to her by family and society. While their journeys are unique, they are also universal, in that young adults across generations seek independence and belonging. In Part III we will look at the *Center Points* exercises in the domains of Balance,

Belonging, Focus, and Meaning as a model for increasing social and emotional success in young adulthood.

It is normal for the life-stage of emerging adulthood to be a time of great flux. Emerging adults may be working on resolving earlier stages of psychosocial development and at the same time forging ahead toward more advanced human aspirations. The four *Center Points* domains, Balance, Belonging, Focus, and Meaning, categorize the skills that are pertinent to successful resolution of the teen years and transitioning into full adulthood. The exercises provide practical tools for working through social anxiety, balancing the nervous system, managing moods, mastering impulsivity, fostering wholesome habits, finding meaningful employment, building community, building self-compassion and, ultimately, building compassion for others.

The following chart summarizes the Western and Eastern disciplines explored in Part I and Part II, and will help with choosing a starting place within the *Center Points* exercises. For example, an emerging adult like Jake who is struggling with making important decisions and regulating emotions, might start with the Focus exercises in Chapter 7, to help with an overwhelmed distracted mind. A mentor working with a emerging adult like Darcy who is struggling with safe, intimate connections can turn to the *Center Points* exercises in Chapter 6 that address Belonging. Young adults, like Tracey, who are overwhelmed by their options or feeling dominated by familial or societal expectations might look at the exercises found in Chapter 8, that help define values.

The *Center Points* Model for Well-being

Center Points Domain	Corresponding Buddhist quality	Most useful for emerging adults struggling with	Corresponding developmental virtue	Other helpful contemplative practices	Relevant theories from Western psychology
Balance	Equanimity	Basic self-care, basic safety, anxiety or depression	Hope, will, purpose	Yamas and Niyamas, Ansanas and Pranyamas found in the Eightfold Path of classical yoga	Theories that embrace mind/body awareness like mindfulness-based cognitive therapy, DBT
Belonging	Equanimity, loving-kindness, compassion (especially toward self)	Connecting with peers, managing relationships with parents or other mentors, forging strong relationships	Purpose, competence, fidelity, mutuality	Following the Yamas and Niyamas, and studying the idea of union found in classical yoga	Attachment theory, humanistic theories, family systems
Focus	Equanimity, loving-kindness, compassion, empathetic joy	Choosing a path, making decisions in work or love, or feeling overwhelmed by social media or other technology	Competence, fidelity, will, purpose	Classical yoga theory, Pratyahara, Dharana, Dhyana.	MBCT, other mindfulness-based practices
Meaning	Compassion, empathetic joy	Finding inspiration, meaningful employment, and like-minded community	Care, wisdom	Following the Yamas and Niyamas, and studying the idea of union found in classical yoga	Positive psychology, MBCT, humanistic theories.

Honor your learning style

As you will see, the exercises in Part III offer a broad array of mindfulness-based practices (MBPs). Meditation purists may think that we have stretched the definition of mindfulness a bit too far. However, Jon Kabat-Zinn, et al. (2016), defines mindfulness-based practices as having these components:

1. Mindfulness-based practices are based on the intersection of contemplative traditions and science, and are often applied to medicine, psychology, or education.
2. These practices address causes of human distress and the pathways to relieving it.
3. Mindfulness practices develop a new relationship with experience and thought through present-moment focus.
4. They promote attentional, emotional, and behavioral self-regulation, as well as positive qualities such as equanimity, compassion, loving-kindness, and joy.

With this definition of MBPs in mind, review the seven categories of learning styles

Keep your learning style in mind as you read through and chose exercises in Part III:

1. Visual-spatial: These learners prefer pictures, images, and spatial understanding. They benefit from using videos, colors, journaling, free writing, or visually organizing information with diagrams.
2. Auditory-musical: Auditory learners enjoy taking in knowledge through sound whether watching a TED talk, listening to music, chanting, or practicing a guided meditation from the latest mindfulness app.
3. Verbal/linguistic: Verbal learners enjoy taking in new information through speaking and writing and will enjoy exercises that involve journaling, mind mapping, and group discourse.

4. Physical/kinesthetic: These learners like to be in motion. They will learn best through mindful movement and hands-on activities.

5. Solitary/intrapersonal: These learners prefer to learn alone. They like to explore the connection between their internal experience and the experience of others in solitude. They may enjoy silent retreats and meditating alone.

6. Social/interpersonal: These learners love group activities and may like to form a discussion group that focuses on mindfulness practices.

7. Logical/mathematical: Logical learners may enjoy memorizing the traditions behind modern mindfulness and may want to go deeper into the Buddhist, yogic, or other contemplative texts. Start by memorizing the Eightfold Path or the Eight Limbs of Yoga. Compare how modern scientific studies confirm the benefits of these traditions.

A precious garland

Start where you are. There is no precise order to the four categories of Balance, Belonging, Focus, and Meaning. The Eight Limbs of yoga have been compared to a precious garland. When one flower on a garland is lifted the others follow. The same is true with the *Center Points* exercises. Mentors and emerging adults can trust that practicing any of the following exercises will enhance well-being and will find that each of the four *Center Points* categories enhance the other three, creating a virtuous cycle – a positive path. As you work your way through the exercises, remember that they are practices. The best results will be achieved by returning to them, like the present moment, again and again. To track your practice you may find it helpful to keep a centering journal – a plain notebook or bound journal where you record your *Center Points* practices each day and make note of the effects the practices have on your thoughts and actions on a daily basis. Review of the journal will help you discern which practices work best for you.

CHAPTER 5

Balance

*Grounding in the body to grow
in equanimity and resiliency*

Think back to Isabel who we met in Chapter 1. She became increasingly unmotivated and physiologically out of balance after dropping out of college and moving back in with her parents. The exercises in this chapter focus on regaining balance by teaching emerging adults stress reduction skills, grounding them in their present surroundings, and helping them make the important connection between daily routines and health. They are designed to reset an overwhelmed nervous system so emerging adults are then free to focus on finding strong social connections, and meaningful, sustainable work. Emerging adults like Isabel will have an easier time rediscovering motivation and happiness after anxiety, stress, and low energy are addressed, and routines that foster self-confidence are established.

What areas in your life could benefit from a little more balance? Journal your thoughts in your centering journal.

Center Points on Balance

These are the Center Points exercises you will find in this chapter.

- Breathing for Balance
- Mood Mapping: Catch a mood before it catches you
- Basic Self-Care: The three-day rolling average system
- Real Food – The best medicine for your brain
- Physical Exercise for Emotional Well-being
- Why Sleep
- Find Your Center: Cultivate the opposite
- Wabi Sabi Imperfection – Balancing self-improvement and self-care
- What is Your Money Type
- Mindful Media Consumption – Who's in control, you or Facebook
- Creating a Personal Vision of Well-being
- Decision Making 101

Breathing for Balance

Goals:
- Understanding the basics of the stress response
- Learning a basic breathing exercise to restore mental and physical balance

The Benefits of Mindfulness Meditation and Conscious Breathing. No matter what our personal stress style, all human bodies respond physically to stress in the same way. Fortunately we have some simple and free tools at our disposal to help us counter the stress response. These tools can be practiced anywhere! Deep breathing allows us to access the underutilized rest and digest response. This response causes blood pressure to decrease and slows the heart rate. Gastric juices are released so that the body can digest and absorb the maximum amount of nutrition available in food.

The opposite of the rest and digest response is the overutilized fight or flight response. In fight or flight mode, the heart rate increases, pupils dilate, and blood flow is rushed to the limbs to help us escape danger. This response happens whether the stressful situation is at work or at home; whether it is real or imagined.

The fight or flight response helps us remove ourselves from dangerous situations. Problems occur when these stress reactions happen too frequently and/or too close together. Then occasional stress becomes chronic stress. The body is then bombarded with stress hormones such as cortisol, and we run the risk of developing conditions such as sleep disorders, depression, heart disease, and chronic fatigue, among others. Stress can make us more vulnerable to illness and can prematurely age us. How we respond to chronic stress – going for a walk as opposed to smoking, for instance – will ultimately slow down or speed up these unwanted processes.

Mindful Breathing and other mindfulness practices help you to achieve moment to moment awareness in a non-judgmental, detached way, thereby increasing the amount of time per day spent in rest and digest mode. Conscious attention to breathing is common in many forms of meditation and is used by top athletes to enhance performance. Why not start treating yourself like a top athlete and try this peak performance tool?

Exercise:

- Sit in a comfortable position either on a chair with your feet on the ground, or on the floor with your legs comfortably crossed. Sit tall with your spine extended so that your breath can enter your entire torso. Relax your shoulders down and move your shoulder blades towards each other.
- Place one hand on your abdomen and the other above your chest near your collarbone.
- Inhale deeply from the bottom of your abdomen. Feel the expansion pressing against your lower hand.
- Continue to fill your torso until you feel the hand on your upper chest expand. Hold the breath for one second.
- Release the breath from the chest to the abdomen. Picture a cup of water emptying from the top to the bottom as you exhale. Note how it feels to be empty of breath just for a second before your next inhale, then repeat this long, slow even breath nine more times. Return to the breath count as your mind wanders, which it naturally will.
- Return to natural breathing. Take a moment to stretch, and write about your experience in your centering journal. Don't worry if mindful breathing feels awkward or uncomfortable. It will feel more natural the more you practice. Remember, these are muscle responses. You can't throw a football like Tom Brady or play the trumpet like Wynton Marsalis right off the bat, either. Practice, practice, practice.

Mood Mapping: Catch a mood before it catches you

Goal:
- Understanding the connection between thoughts and mood

Uncomfortable/less pleasant............Pleasant/joyful feelings
1 – 2 – 3 – 4 – 5 – 6 – 7 – 8 – 9 – 10

The previous exercise is designed to calm and center your nervous system, and therefore your entire physical being. If we pair these powerful breathing practices with watching our thoughts, we start to have more control over the emotional being (the mind) that can lead to unhelpful moods. By watching our thoughts we begin to trust the simple truth that all mood states are impermanent. This is an important practice for anyone in transition, when we sometimes lose perspective and assign too much meaning to passing moods.

Exercise:

- **Set a timer** on your phone, computer, or watch to remind yourself to watch your thoughts three times each day, and chart their impact on mood.

- **Morning mindfulness:** Start every day this week with five minutes of *Breathing for Balance* or five to ten minutes of gentle movement. Keep this exercise to five minutes or less so that you stay motivated to practice. Use your centering journal to chart your mood at the beginning of the day. Take a few moments to consider the impermanence of your mood. Think about the last time your mood was slightly more positive. Chances are it was not too long ago. Create a simple scale to chart the level of pleasure or discomfort you are feeling similar to the one above. For example: This morning I'm feeling a little nervous about my commute to work – I'm closer to the bottom of the uncomfortable/pleasant scale. I'd say I'm at 3.

- **Mid-day break:** Start with *Breathing for Balance*. Check your mood. Are you still at a 3 on the uncomfortable/pleasant scale? Or did you swing toward pleasure once you found yourself at your desk and organized your work for the day? Record your results in your journal. For example: The morning traffic was heavy, but when I got to work I had a few minutes to get some coffee and chat with my co-worker. I'm at about 6 on the uncomfortable/pleasant scale now.

- **In the evening:** Once again reset your nervous system with balanced breathing, and then map your mood on the uncomfortable/pleasant scale. If you find yourself on or under 5, use your journal to park any worrying thoughts for the evening. If sleep is difficult come up with a positive thought about sleep and write it in your journal. For example: It's okay for me to rest now. Rest helps me integrate my day. Over time, paying attention to my stress level will improve my sleep.

This exercise helps us recognize that our mood states are impermanent. It builds confidence in our ability to move our mood towards more episodes of contentment. With consistent practice we can turn contentment from a temporary state to a lasting personal trait.

Basic Self-Care: The three-day rolling average system

Goals:
- Identifying the foundations of self-care and their connection to mindfulness
- Developing a plan to incorporate nourishing food as well as adequate amounts of sleep and exercise into a busy week

The three pillars of basic self-care are diet, sleep, and exercise. Attending to all three pillars is essential for peak brain activity which will help with maintaining a good mood and making good decisions. Ideally, we would all be eating a diet comprised of nutritious food every day, exercising for at least twenty minutes, and sleeping 7-8 hours a night. But the ideal and the real often clash, especially when we are in transition.

Exercise:

Instead of making basic self-care another stressor during already stressful periods, try the three-day rolling average check-in as outlined below.

- Think back on the last three days and answer the following questions in your centering journal:
  1. **What kind of real food (food that can be grown vs. processed food) did I eat in the last three days?** *Sample answer: I've been really good about eating protein and fruit at breakfast ... I can't remember the last time I had a vegetable though ....*

2. **What kind of physical activity/exercise did I get in the last three days?** *Sample answer: Feeling good about this category! I've been walking with a co-worker at lunch every day!*

3. **How much sleep did I get over the last three nights?** *Sample answer: Not so great. I've been getting an average of five hours per night. I was out late with friends Saturday and Sunday. I drank a lot of coffee on Monday and had trouble sleeping on Monday night.*

- **Based on your three-day rolling average, which component of basic self-care (diet, exercise, sleep) do you want to focus on today? Be sure to make these goals real and measureable.** *Sample answer: It's Tuesday afternoon. I have a plan to cook chicken and broccoli stir-fry with my roommate tonight. I'm going to plan to get into bed with a book by 10:00 pm.*

- **Continue to update your three-day rolling average for the next twenty-one days. Record your averages in you centering journal. What changes did you notice? Which of the three basic self-care components affect your decision-making the most? (Everyone is different.)** *Sample answers: I noticed that if I don't get some kind of fresh food at least once a day, my stomach starts to really bother me…. If I only get to work out every third day, I feel okay, but I noticed I just can't skimp on sleep during the week.*

Remember, the IDEAL is to get all three basic self-care components every day, but the three-day rolling average can help prevent burn-out and emotional set-backs.

Real Food – The best medicine for your brain

Goals:
- Understanding the connection between good nutrition and healthy brain functioning
- Exploring easy and economical sources of unprocessed whole food

Real food provides vitamins and nutrients that processed foods and pharmaceuticals just don't. Nutrition fads and facts are changing all the time. Here are some tried and true real food facts to motivate you to incorporate real food into your diet and some easy ways to make it happen every day.

Exercise:

After learning about economical sources of unprocessed whole food, plan a trip to your favorite grocery store. Challenge yourself to try at least two recipes that contain the nutrients listed below. Take a few deep breaths before you eat your meals. Remember that deep breathing will help activate the rest and digest response, helping you to absorb, and enjoy your meals.

We are fatheads – The human brain is made up predominantly of fat that we can only get from our diet. We need these sources of good Omega 3 fatty acids like EPA and DHA for maximum brain function.

> **Easy source:** Fish oil is easily assimilated by the human body and a healthy source of good fatty acids. However it can be expensive and hard to ingest. Ground flaxseed is less pricey per serving, readily available and can be mixed into a morning smoothie, oatmeal, or applesauce, and sprinkled into soup or salad. Most nuts and seeds also contain omega-3s and are a great snack choice.

115

Protein is not optional – Without a food source of protein, we can't produce serotonin and dopamine – two major players in mood and brain health. It's best to get a little protein at every meal.

> **Easy source:** Breakfast – make time for low-sugar yogurt or a handful of nuts. Lunch – Turkey slices, or a scoop of peanut or almond butter. Dinner – small catch fish (salmon, trout) or chicken. For vegetarians, beans, soy products, or cheese, are easy ingredients to mix with rice and veggies.

Manage stress with B vitamins – Stress increases the body's need for B vitamins. When B is low, we can't convert food to energy. Some people have a genetic tendency to have trouble with this conversion, and may need supplementation. Start with your diet, and consult with your doctor about supplementation.

> **Easy source:** Quick power salad with roasted veggies: Slice some root veggies like beets, potatoes, and squash and spread them in a baking dish. Sprinkle with olive oil, salt and pepper. (Mindfulness tip: Take a second to enjoy the color of this dish). Bake at 400 degrees until tender. Meanwhile boil an egg or two (or more if you want extras for tomorrow's breakfast). Slice up your favorite greens and toss with olive oil, vinegar or lemon juice. Top greens with roasted veggies, chopped eggs, and avocado.

Magnesium (and other mineral) madness – Are you feeling the kind of physical stress that manifests itself as tight muscles, cramps, constipation, or insomnia? It's likely that magnesium can help. Many factors can make it hard to get enough minerals in our diet. Again, try food sources for these nutrients, but if you are experiencing some of the above symptoms, magnesium can be absorbed through the skin by Epsom salt baths. The pill form of magnesium is an inexpensive and easy-to-find supplement.

> **Easy source:** We all have time for this one: dark chocolate! Pair this with pumpkin seeds for an on-the-go source.

Grate dark chocolate and melt into cow or nut milk for a healthy, yummy snack. Leafy greens (although not sprinkled with chocolate) are also a great source of a full spectrum of minerals.

One more worth mentioning: Vitamin D can be obtained through salmon and mackerel as well as fortified dairy products, but one of the easiest ways to get vitamin D is by soaking up the sun.

Easy source: Twenty minutes a day in the sunshine can help boost mood and energy. If you have concerns about low vitamin D levels affecting you mood, ask your doctor for a simple blood test and appropriate levels of supplementation.

Physical Exercise for Emotional Well-being

Goals:
- Understanding the connection between physical exercise and mental clarity
- Building motivation to make physical exercise a habit

You may be motivated to exercise in pursuit of a certain body type. But one of the best benefits of regular exercise is that it increases the experience of positive emotions and makes your mind and body more resilient to stress.

Exercise:

Here are some mood-related motivating tidbits that will help you incorporate exercise into your self-care routine. Try one or more a week for the next month. Record your mood changes (as opposed to body changes) in your centering journal.

- The term *stress inoculation* describes the process of inducing small amounts of stress for the sake of building resiliency. You may be familiar with how this idea works on your muscles, but did you know it works on your mind too? Even a short burst of exercise registers as stress in the brain. After the short burst of exercise, during the recovery phase, your brain says, "Hey, I survived that!" Then, the next time you feel physical or mental stress, say a meeting with your boss, you will have more resiliency against the fight or flight response.

    Try this: Take a run around your neighborhood for ten minutes right now, or do two sets of 25-50 jumping jacks. Did you survive? Do you feel more calm and clear-headed?

- You may be a digital native, working behind a screen or desk, but your nervous system is stuck in the Stone Age and has not caught up with rapid cultural evolution. The nervous system is the same model that our Paleo ancestors had, and is still designed to keep the body as alert and active as when food supplies were scarce and required a lot of time and energy to find.

    Try this: Treat your physical body like a caveperson's when gathering food. When you go to a grocery store, convenience store, or restaurant, park further away than necessary. If it's safe and well lit, take a lap or two around the parking lot. This is an easy way to add more steps into your weekly routine, and a reminder that the human nervous system has some serious catching up to do before it is designed to be as sedentary as our modern lifestyle.

- Exercise helps tryptophan and BDNF (a protein that encourages new brain cell growth) to cross the blood-brain barrier. The result: production of serotonin, the neurotransmitter that boosts mood, manages anxiety, impulsivity, and assists in learning.

    Try this: Choose a book or an article on a new topic. Read four pages before exercising, then read four more after twenty minutes of rigorous movement. Did you notice a difference in your ability to pay attention?

- GABA (gamma-aminobutyric acid), the brain's major inhibitory transmitter, increases with exercise. GABA puts the breaks on (inhibits) the fight or flight response, and is the main target for many anti-anxiety drugs. GABA calms the mind down enough to take in positive experiences.

    Try this: Get your heart rate up with a 20-minute brisk walk, a 10-minute run, or two sets of fifty jumping jacks. Notice the contents of your thoughts before and after. Are they slightly more positive post-exercise? Even if you are worried about an upcoming event, do you feel more in control?

- We all have a different stress set-point. It is a product of our genetic code and environmental exposure to stress, we all have a different threshold for switching on the fight or flight response. The good news is exercise helps to raise the trigger point of the physical and mental response to stress.

  Try this: Practice ten to twenty minutes of aerobic exercise every day this week, or forty minutes three times a week, whichever best fits into your schedule. After a week, notice your reaction to a typical stressor, like getting stuck in traffic, social stress, or a heavy workload.

Why Sleep?

Goals:
- Building a healthy relationship with sleep
- Creating a bedtime ritual that promotes healthy sleep

All things in the natural world have rhythms and routines. Consider the phases of the moon, the waves of the ocean, the seasons of the year. Humans, too, have rhythms. Unlike the rest of the natural world, we often work against the natural cycle of work and rest by denying our bodies and brains enough sleep every night.

Exercise:

Read through the following sleep facts that will motivate you to take sleep more seriously. This week, try one or two sleep tips designed to help you develop a friendlier attitude toward sleep. Record your results in your centering journal.

- **Sleep fact:** Memory consolidation – the ability to learn and record new ideas – is greatly enhanced by a good night's sleep, as is our ability to be creative. This is the science behind the phrase, Let me sleep on it. During sleep, neuronal pruning takes place, helping us shed neuro-networks that we no longer use, experience mental clarity, and make better decisions.

    Sleep tip: The next time you have a big decision to make, write down a summary of the situation. Place the summary away from your sleep area. Ask sleep to help you with the answer. In the morning notice if you slept better and have more clarity. By following this process, chances are good that you will come up with a creative answer to your problem.

- **Sleep fact:** Ghrelin, the hunger hormone, is released when we are sleep deprived. When we deprive our body of sleep, the nervous system receives a stress signal, making us hungrier.

  Sleep tip: Going to bed with a stomach that is too full or too empty may disturb your sleep. An hour before bed, have a small, easy to digest snack, like a small bowl of yogurt, whole-wheat toast, or a glass of warm milk.

- **Sleep fact:** Studies show that one night of poor sleep inhibits the immune system by 25 to 30%. Take note of the connection between your seasonal allergies and colds and your good sleep habits.

  Sleep tip: Note in your journal how many hours you slept. At the end of the day enter how your seasonal allergies and/ or colds felt. Note the correlation between adequate sleep and how your body reacts to outside stimuli such as pollen.

- **Sleep fact:** Experimenting with your ideal sleep schedule is an essential part of getting quality rest.

  Sleep tip: Try to go to sleep and wake up as close as possible to the same time each day. If this seems boring or unsustainable, try adjusting your sleep/wake times to something that works for you.

- **Sleep fact:** Shaking off physical and mental stress at the end of each day will lead to better sleep.

  Sleep tip: Practice gentle stretching to release the day's tension before you get into bed. Take note of one or two accomplishments of your day in your centering journal. Resist the natural tendency of noting what's left on the to-do list.

- **Sleep fact:** Make your room a sleep sanctuary by limiting activity.

  Sleep tip: Keep your room cool, dark, and quiet. If noise and light are a problem, try earplugs and an eye mask. Break the habit of falling asleep in front of a screen. The blue light from electronics sends a signal to the brain to stay awake. Instead, get into bed and take some long, slow breaths with extra-long exhales. Relax all the muscles in your body staring at your feet, think about feeling heavy and relaxed. Welcome sleep!

Find Your Center: Cultivate the opposite

Goal:
- Finding alternatives to self-defeating patterns

When we feel out of balance, we often resort to go-to habits that keep us stuck. An example of this might be, "I went over my budget again this month. Maybe I can get a loan, or buy groceries on my credit card."

While these external behaviors might be necessary, and even adaptive, they are often like putting a finger into the crumbling wall of a dam. Cultivating the opposite in thought, word, and action, can help you make lasting behavioral change that extends beyond the problem at hand. Here's how it works.

Exercise:

Answer the following questions to help you start thinking in terms of opposite action. Then look at the example below to help you get a sense of how cultivating the opposite can help you find your center.

- In thought – what thoughts or emotions are causing you to lose balance – What would be an opposite thought or emotion?
- In word – have you caught yourself agreeing to someone else's plan? – What would be an opposite response? Can you find a response that takes self-care into consideration?
- In habit - have you noticed unwanted patterns creeping in? How would you pull yourself back to the middle by cultivating the opposite? Choose one pattern, like

overspending, overreacting, or procrastination, and cultivate the opposite for the next month.

- Journal about these three areas. How might you have restated something to achieve an outcome fair to yourself and the person with whom you are speaking?

The following example of cultivating the opposite will help you get started.

Thought: What are your thoughts about the situation? "If I don't go out to the expensive dinner with my friends they wouldn't ask me the next time." "I can't believe I went over my budget again, what is my problem!"

Cultivate the opposite: Instead of self-criticism, cultivate understanding: "I actually know a lot of people who struggle with their budget. I know it takes practice." "The next time I'm worried about missing out, I can call a friend and do something together that we can both afford."

Word: "When my friend asked me out to the dinner, I was uncomfortable, but I said 'sure' even though in my gut I knew I would be over extending myself. But I felt compelled to make a fast decision."

Cultivate the opposite: "I could have said, that sounds like a blast… Let me think about it." Unless someone is dying and you hold the key to his or her survival, you can always use this phrase. It will help you cultivate the opposite of impulsivity – namely discernment, or thoughtful decision-making. With discernment you give yourself time and might come up with a response such as, "How about if I come at the end of the meal for coffee?" This is a thoughtful, authentic response that takes your own needs into account.

Habit: Here's where the follow-through comes into play. "It felt good to meet up with those friends at the end of the meal. I was a little uncomfortable, but I was true to myself, and I have more money for groceries this week! I might even share this idea with a close friend so we can practice together."

Wabi Sabi Imperfection: Balancing self-improvement and self-care

Goals:
- Noticing the loneliness that comes about by constantly pursuing perfection
- Finding an alternative to perfection that fosters well-being and still allows for achieving goals

You are not a perpetual self-improvement project. You are a miracle of nature. And like all of nature, you are imperfect. In fact, being human assumes imperfection. Sure, there are times that we want to put forth our best effort and to excel, especially in the emerging adult years. But perpetual perfection is for inanimate objects. Ask a marble statue how it feels, and it will probably tell you it is pretty bored and lonely.

Exercise:

Use the Japanese philosophy of Wabi Sabi to make peace with imperfection. Wabi Sabi adheres to these four principles:

- Everything is unfinished
- Everything is imperfect
- Everything is impermanent
- Everything is connected

Consider the following scenarios, and then apply them to your own life:

Everything is imperfect. Wabi Sabi philosophy asks us to see the beauty in the natural world. At my home in New Hampshire I look out on a pine tree that has two tops like a tuning fork. There's a part of me that is a little annoyed by this tree. A voice that says, "That doesn't look right." But ultimately the tree serves as a gentle reminder of "perfect imperfection," and unique beauty. It's not as if I can just go out there and fix it, the way I might fluff a pillow on a couch. Is there an imperfection in your life that sometimes eats away at your happiness? Can you allow yourself to see the beauty in the unique? This week, notice the beautiful imperfection of the natural world.

Everything is unfinished. In my private counseling practice I work with many students from a local music conservatory. Conservatory life, by its very nature, encourages pursuit of excellence. There is nothing wrong with this. However, I have seen many students lose their love of music by confusing excellence with perfection. The philosophy and life style of Wabi Sabi has often helped them reconnect with the joy of music. The idea of everything being unfinished can be revelatory to young adults who want to make their mark. What is finished? Who can tell us? Can Beethoven? Mozart? At some point we need to put down the instrument, the computer program, the plan, and rest in the unfinished. This week, find a project, an idea, or burning desire that you can put down for a while, unfinished.

Everything is impermanent. This is both a relief, and a sorrow. Things and people evolve and change. In New England, unbearably hot summer days turn into crisp autumn splendor. The beauty of a snow-filled field turns into the transition season of early spring known as mud season. Nothing is static or fixed, even our work and our greatest love will always be changing and evolving. Sometimes there is gain, sometimes there is loss, but holding on too tight to a certain outcome can cause suffering. This week, talk with a friend about an impermanent situation in your life. Can you find the right amount of holding? Not too tight and not too loose?

Everything is connected. Wabi Sabi celebrates the rustic, sparse solitude of nature. It's not a disconnection, but actually a solitude that leads us to deeper connection. By embracing the idea that the natural world (including you!) is wonderfully unfinished, perfectly imperfect, and ever-changing, you can more comfortably connect with the rest of the Wabi Sabi tribe. This week notice how much easier it is to connect with peers when you accept your (and their) imperfection.

What Is Your Money Type?

Goals:
- Building an awareness around the causes of your spending habits
- Changing self-defeating habits, and cultivating a balanced, healthy relationship with money

Feeling good about your finances is not just a matter of checks and balances. Understanding your emotional relationship with money is essential.

Exercise:

Take a look at the following money types. Although not many people fit into one type, this tool can help you understand some of your attitudes towards money and help you identify areas that are keeping you from spending too much or earning too little. Check those that apply to you.

The Spender. Spenders are those who buy beyond their means. These individuals need to look closely at the connection between shopping and mood so they don't use shopping as a drug.

- I often buy things that are not budgeted for.
- When I do create a budget, I have a hard time sticking to it.
- I often make purchases immediately after seeing an advertisement for a product.
- I spend a lot of time thinking about shopping.
- I am worried about my credit card debt.

The Hoarder. Hoarders cling to money in an unnecessary way. They may have a fear of poverty even though they face no real threat. Hoarders actually create the daily experience of poverty because of their discomfort with uncertainty.

- I spend a lot of time worrying about losing my income.
- I experienced financial instability as a child.
- I will often go without necessities like reliable transportation for work or nutritious food.

The Money Hater. Money haters believe that money is the root of all evil. They might make broad, negative generalizations about wealthy people. Money haters often feel superior to others by doing without or creating conditions of poverty. Money haters have a strong moral sense that money is inherently bad. They may have a fear of success that they cover up by preaching about the evils of money.

- I tend to feel satisfied or superior to others when I forego a necessity.
- I have strong feelings about wealthy people or people who buy luxury items.
- I have turned down opportunities to increase my income.

The Money Chaser. The money chaser puts high priority on acquiring a fortune. Money chasers are often looking for the next big break and can be quick to jump on the bandwagon of the latest money making scheme. They tend to admire or envy wealthy individuals. They may make risky investments with their own or other's life savings.

- I tend to ignore financial advice from experts.
- I have started a business without a business plan.
- I believe that if I just had some start-up cash, it would change my life.

- My investment ideas have caused problems with important relationships.

What messages did you get from your family of origin that influence your money type?

- Think of money as something we exchange for our life energy. Are you earning and spending money in a manner that is worth the exchange of your life energy? Changing unhealthy habits about money takes time as money views are often deeply ingrained. Getting curious about your attitudes is the first step to changing them and can help you develop a healthier money type that might sound something like this:

The Healthy Money Mind:
- I try to take care of my basic needs before buying things that are not necessary.
- I know how to enjoy myself without spending a lot.
- I understand that there are two ways to build savings: Spending less and/or increasing my income.
- I accept that managing money is part of life. I'm willing to ask for advice, or talk to a financial planner.

Mindful Media Consumption: Who's in control, you or social media?

> **Goals:**
> - Looking at the many ways that technology enhances life
> - Building an awareness of times when technology is stealing joy

Used properly, technology can help us live more streamlined lives and have less cluttered minds. Too often, however, we seem to be taken over by technology, becoming less aware of the here and now.

Exercise:

Get together with friends and create a "mindful tech team." Use these tips to balance your relationship with your hi-tech gadgets:

- Practice unitasking: Try to use one piece of technology at a time. Resist the urge to watch your TV while surfing the web. Avoid listening to phone messages and checking email at the same time. The multitasking myth has been officially blown open. Studies show that multitasking actually slows productivity, and it adds wear and tear on your nervous system. When using technology, use one gadget at a time. **Mindful tech tip:** Breathe deep and enjoy one piece of tech at a time. Instead of using your smartphone when you are watching a movie, watch your breath instead. Take a break from the movie if need be to check messages, but notice if it is difficult to unitask with technology. Share your experience with a friend.

- Designate time: We lose time to technology when we get in the habit of repetitively and mindlessly checking email or text messages.
  Mindful tech tip: Have designated times throughout the day for returning phone calls, and checking emails. Try once in the morning, and once late afternoon. Let friends and colleagues know that this is your policy so others will know that you don't always respond on demand.

- Download timeout software: Conduct research on the great smart phone applications and meditation software programs that can be set at intervals throughout the day to remind you to take a break.
  Mindful tech tip: Appendix A includes a list of apps that help you schedule down time with guided meditations. Find an hour this week to review these apps with your tech team. Chose one to download. Rate your success with each app you try. It may seem counterintuitive, but sometimes technology really does help us manage our time with technology!

- Take a tech-free day once every month, or at least half of a day:
  Mindful tech tip: This is an advanced skill! It's okay if you slip and check your texts. The idea is to remember what it's like to live without being bombarded with the distraction of technology. Does the thought of this make your skin crawl? Grab your tech team for support.

- Social media-free day: Yes, you read that right.
  Mindful tech tip: If you can't take an entire day away from email or texting because of work or family commitments, take the social media-free day challenge. Is it difficult for you to be out of the loop in this way? Maybe life without social media is a relief? Notice what comes up for you when you resist logging in.

- Use technology to foster gratitude:
  Mindful tech tip: Email or text someone with the intention of being thankful. Express gratitude for having them in your life.

- Get honest about comparing: Notice if comparing yourself to others on social media is bringing you down.
  Mindful tech tip: Talk to your tech team about where you struggle to stay balanced with technology. Have an honest conversation about how social media affects your mood, your productivity, and daily life satisfaction. Support each other in your attempts to use media to boost connection as opposed to boosting stress.

- Be kind to yourself as you work to change your technology habit: It takes persistence to change habits so be gentle with yourself if you backslide.
  Mindful tech tip: It can help to make a list of the pros and cons of using and overusing technology. It can also help to notice your stress level after a few days of cutting back on technology.

Creating a Personal Vision of Well-being

Goals:
- Exploring the multi-faceted concept of well-being
- Making a personal well-being plan with a well-being collage

Exercise:

Take some centering breaths, and then read through the following definitions of well-being. Proceed to the collage exercise and personalize a vision of well-being.

Definitions:
- Well-being is the overall state of feeling content, healthy, and connected.
- Well-being is a choice – a decision you make to move toward optimal health.
- Well-being is a way of life – a lifestyle you design to achieve your highest potential.
- Well-being is a process – This process requires developing awareness around many domains of health. There is no end point, only a movement toward, or away from well-being. Even so, well-being can only be experienced in the present moment. It is just a breath away.
- Well-being is a balanced channeling of energy – energy received from the environment, transformed within you, and returned to affect the world around you.
- Well-being is the integration of body, mind, and spirit – the appreciation that everything you do, and think, and feel, and believe has an impact on your state of health, and the health of the world.

- Well-being is a holistic and preventative measure of health that takes into account the physical, mental, and social domains of an individual life. Some domains are easier for us to change than others, but we always have control over some aspects of our well-being.

Well-being collage:

Think about a time in your life when you felt satisfied and happy with the way your life was going. In other words, a time you felt "well." Name two or three activities or components of this time. What do you feel contributed most to your sense of wellness? What would you need to do to recreate this environment? Create a collage from magazines, photos, or your own art. Make sure the collage contains symbols of each activity or component. After making your collage write down two or three precise goals that will invite well-being back into your life.

Here's an example:

- I felt great when I was training for a 5-mile race with my friend. I'm going to find another race and recruit some friends to train with me.
- I felt a sense of balance when I was visiting my family once a month. I'm going to call my siblings to see if they can meet for dinner this month.
- I can remember a time when I was not on social media for two hours a day. I'm going to make a plan to talk my friends face-to-face at least once a day.
- Hang your collage in place where you will see it every day.

Decision Making 101

Goals:
- Enhancing the ability to take time making decisions
- Exploring ways to build the skill of discernment

Discernment, defined as "the ability to judge well," is an important life skill. Yet many of the models for a life well-lived found in Eastern and Western contemplative traditions ask us to keep an open and flexible mind. How do we strike a balance between open-mindedness and a sense of discernment that keeps us safe from harm, especially in emerging adulthood, when we are just starting to make truly important, independent decisions?

Exercise:

Identify an important decision that needs to be made. Read through the following tools that support good decision-making. Share your thinking process with someone you trust. Sometimes well-meaning friends or family members are too invested in the outcome of your decision to be objective. If that is the case, ask a trusted mentor to help you talk through the decision-making process.

Balancing logic and intuition. When making an important decision, make sure to engage both sides of the brain. It may seem like the best solution includes only factual information, but studies show that we make better decisions when we also employ intuition, the felt sense or more emotion-based sense of the right path. One way to enhance logic is to make a pros/cons list. One way to enhance intuition is to envision each choice and notice your bodily reaction to each visualization.

Patience. By taking your time to make a big decision (as much time as is available), you will be giving yourself time for ideas to "percolate," especially if you take the time to quiet your mind and focus on the breath, or some other relaxing but healthy distraction.

Open-mindedness and flexibility. Watch out for first reactions like, "absolutely not!" With a rigid stance, you may be making decisions based solely on old fears and failures.

Compassion. Are you applying discernment to a relationship? Compassion is key. We all need to balance giving someone the benefit of the doubt, giving a situation some time, and cutting our losses when our needs are not being met. Combine logic and intuition with compassion. For example, if a friend stood you up for the second time in a row, is it time to reconsider the relationship, or is she currently going through a tough time that calls for a more compassionate response?

Remember your values. After all the components of discernment have been explored, don't forget to check in with your values. Is your decision in line with your values statement (see Chapter 8). One way to tell, when you think about the results of your decision, does it make you feel energized or depleted?

Summary:

It will take some time for the human nervous system to catch up with the accelerated pace of change. To thrive in the 21st Century we need to keep in mind the needs of our physical body. By doing so, it will be easier to access calm mood states, and feel more at ease in interpersonal settings. Which *Center Points* balance exercises will you add to your week? The next chapter provides exercises that help young adults build healthy communication skills and close relationships.

CHAPTER 6

Belonging

*Compassion for self and others is essential
for building intimacy and community*

Recall the story of Darcy, an emerging adult who is struggling to recover from unhealthy relationship patterns. The belonging exercises in this chapter are designed to help emerging adults see self-compassion and compassion toward others as important social skills. Remember that fMRI imaging confirms that compassion-based contemplative exercises make visible changes in the structure of the brain. Self-compassion, as opposed to the ever-popular self-loathing, judging, and comparing are what help us make true, lasting connections to friends and romantic partners.

- Can you think of areas in your life where you are too self-critical or critical of others?
- What do you think would happen if you softened just a bit, toward yourself or toward others?

Doing the exercises in this chapter will help you answer these questions.

Center Points on Belonging

These are the Center Points exercises you will find in this chapter.

- Taming Self-consciousness
- Surviving a Friend Gap
- Building a Sense of Place
- How and Why to ask for Help
- Mindful Communication Often Requires Follow-up
- Self-Compassion 101: Why self-compassion will help you connect with others
- Intensity Versus Intimacy in a Romantic Relationship
- Mindfulness for a Broken Heart
- Visualization to Help Calm Social Anxiety
- Switch from Comparing to Connecting
- Fear of Missing Out (FOMO) – And other ways of feeling left behind
- Getting Ready for your Work Evaluation

Taming Self-consciousness

Goals:
- Feeling less isolated in social settings
- Identifying self-defeating thoughts and behaviors

We've all felt it. You're standing at a party or sitting in a meeting at work, and you just feel like an outsider. You might be thinking: They must have made a mistake when they invited me/hired me/ accepted me. These thoughts and feelings are so distracting that your fight or flight response revs up and you start to have trouble contributing to the conversation.

The worst part about this anxious chain reaction is that you feel isolated even though you are in a room full of people.

Exercise:

Memorize the tools listed below before your next social gathering. They will help you tame self-consciousness and encourage genuine, safe, human connection. Just as if you were preparing for an important presentation, practice these tools with a video camera, voice recorder, or trusted friend or mentor.

- **Normalize.** When the demons of self-consciousness take over, we tend to have thoughts like: What is wrong with me? Why can't I just relax.? Although everybody's nervous system is wired differently, all humans are social animals, and social connection is vital for our well-being. Did you know that the area of the brain that registers social rejection is very near the area of the brain that registers physical pain? Ouch! That is why social rejection can feel so threatening. We learn to protect ourselves from any pain, even imagined pain. If you are somebody who has experienced social rejection in the past, as we all have, you might be on guard for the next attack at a party or at work. One of the best ways to tame this misfiring of the nervous system is to bring awareness to the chain-reaction, and correcting the internal dialogue. You might try repeating a phrase like, "Just like me, everyone here wants to be accepted. Just like me, they might feel a little nervous." This kind of normalizing self-talk helps heal and re-wire the brain.

- **Picture the face of a trusted being.** When you find yourself in a stressful social situation, take a few deep breaths, and picture the face of someone you feel entirely comfortable with, someone with whom you can be your true self. This might be an old, dear friend, a family member, or a pet. For some of us this may be the face of a spiritual mentor. Get into the habit of picturing your trusted being before your social event.

- **Get curious.** Trust in the odds that others around you are feeling like outsiders as well. Try switching your focus toward someone else. Is there someone around you who might benefit by being drawn out? Get curious about someone near you. Ask a question about their day. What are they planning to do to relax this weekend? If this person seems nervous, take a deep breath and drop your shoulders, which will encourage them to do the same. Take the focus off of your own stress, and offer someone else the gift of your kind attention.

- **Balance your external desire to impress with your internal intention to connect.** A young lady I work with is a flutist. She, like most musicians, sometimes struggles with performance anxiety. After a particularly miserable performance where she was plagued with self-consciousness, she came close to giving up performing all together. She was scheduled to perform the following week, and to her surprise, this performance went much better and she was able to enjoy the process. When I asked what had changed, she said, "Well, I decided that I prepared the best I could with the time I had. Even so, I can't control others' reactions, so I decided to focus on what I want to express, which is my love of music." Her internal value of sharing her love of music outshone her external desire to impress. What values do you want to carry in your pocket in social situations? (See the exercises in Chapter 8 on finding meaning.)

Normalizing feelings, picturing the face of a friend, getting curious, and being clear about what you want to express versus how you want to impress: Practicing these four tools will help you feel less self-conscious and more connected.

Surviving a Friend Gap

Goals:
- Accepting that social circles change
- Managing a period of time when you have few social outlets

A friend gap is a period of time when you find yourself physically or emotionally distant from friends. This can occur due to relocating, graduating, changing jobs, changes in relationship status, or the natural tendency to change interests during the emerging adult years.

Maybe you just graduated from college or moved out on your own. Maybe your best friend is in a new relationship and is preoccupied. Perhaps your old friend group doesn't appreciate your newfound love of gourmet food or playing the ukulele. There are many reasons you may find yourself in a friend gap. It can be a challenging time where sadness and self-doubt can creep in.

Exercise

Get ready to visualize your ideal social group. But first, identify the thought patterns that often arise when you find yourself in between friends:

- **We have a situation!** A friend gap is situational, not personal. It's about natural change and it is not a permanent state. Watch for and reframe negative self-talk. **Inaccurate self-talk,** "What's wrong with me? Why am I the only one home on a weekend night? There must be something wrong if I've lived here for two months and I haven't found a group. My friend who moved to Texas seems to be making friends." **Accurate self-talk:** "Making friends takes time and commitment. I'll try to plan three activities this week, and strike up three conversations."

- **You are not in exile, although it may feel that way:** When it comes to making new friends, isolation is the enemy. Notice how you feel after a day alone in your new apartment/dorm room. It might feel soothing to reread your favorite novel all day, or to lose yourself on Netflix, or even chat with far-away old friends online, but these can be isolating activities if you are using them to avoid your goal of making new friends. It's time to get curious about the new people around you.

- **What are your friendship strengths?** Before you go out to meet your new friends, it might be helpful to remind yourself of your friendship strengths. What are your top three good qualities when it comes to friendship? Maybe you are adventurous, a good listener, funny? Are you the one who is always planning group activities? If you have trouble coming up with your friend qualities, this is a good time to contact an old friend for help.

- **You have an opportunity! You can be discerning, not desperate.** What kind of friends do you want to surround yourself with? Studies show that our friends, and even our friend's friends, can have a tremendous influence on our behavior. If, in the past, you have followed friends down unhappy roads, now is the time to think about what you want out of your new friends. Do you want to meet people who are more health conscious, more musical, more extroverted? What kinds of associations make you feel good? Only you can answer these questions. Now that you have applied discernment to the situation, it's a time to take a calculated risk. You know your friend gap is not personal, but

147

situational, you have taken stock of your friendship strengths, and you know what kind of people make you feel good.

- **Picture yourself with a group of friends with whom you feel very comfortable.** Take a few centering breaths. What activity are you sharing? How many people are present? Use all your senses to solidify your ideal social scene. How do you feel after you have spent time with this group? Now take a few moments to record the scene in your centering journal.

Building a Sense of Place

> **Goals:**
> - Learning how to feel connected to a place to help ward off loneliness
> - Feeling more at home in a new environment

A sense of belonging doesn't necessarily have to come from other people. You can also foster a greater feeling of belonging by paying attention to a sense of place.

A strong sense of place develops through directly experiencing and learning about a particular area. You can cultivate a sense of place by having direct exposure to the history, geographical features, natural elements, and culture of a place. Developing a sense of place will help you feel connected to a community and less alone even if you are by yourself.

Young adults move a lot. You may have only been in your current community for a year, maybe less. Even moving from one neighborhood to another in the same town can disrupt your sense of place.

Exercise:

Build a deep connection to your surroundings. Start by rereading the above definition of a sense of place. Practice the Breathing for Balance exercises in Chapter 5 for just a few minutes. Start to recall a sense of place from your childhood.

- Use your five senses to recall a special place. Examples: I remember a group of pine trees in my back yard. There were a couple of granite rocks in the center of this circle of trees. I would crawl into the middle and use the fallen pine needles, acorns I found, and other scraps of nature to make fairy houses. The breeze would whisper through the pines blocking out the neighborhood noises, and circulating the smell of the pine needles. I would lose track of time in that place.

- I remember a certain red chair in our town library. It was hidden in a back corner on the upper floor. I was always so happy when that chair was empty. I could read for hours, occasionally looking up to rest my eyes on the dark paneled walls, and to see the light streaming in from the long narrow windows. The librarians got to know me and would always say hello.

- Take a look around your living space or your neighborhood this week. Find little corners that have a sense of familiarity, safety, and peace. Even if you live in the middle of a busy city with five roommates you can cultivate a sense of place at a favorite coffee shop, bakery, park even a small corner of your apartment.

- Make notes in your centering journal about what gives you a sense of belonging through a sense of place.

How and Why to ask for Help

Goals:
- Exploring the idea that asking for help is an important life skill
- Getting more comfortable asking for help and knowing who to ask to increase the chances that you will be successful in receiving what you need

This probably wasn't part of your formal education, but asking for help is an important life skill. It is important because at some point, no matter how independent we are; there will come a time when we need help, when we somehow come up against a natural human limitation. Asking for help can be humbling, but it can also help us connect with our community. Take a few minutes to explore your attitudes and beliefs toward asking for help, the best way to ask for help, and how to give back.

Exercise:

Explore your attitudes and beliefs about asking for help. Then, explore the following tips designed to help you feel more comfortable about asking for help.

Why is it hard for you to ask for help? Which statements apply to you?
- My family holds a strong family value of being self-sufficient.
- My family would ridicule me when I needed help.
- My family was inconsistent about giving me help when I needed it.
- I could always rely on _____ to help me no matter what.

- I don't want to ask for help. Everyone else seems to be doing okay without help.
- I don't want to become dependent on anyone.

As you can see from the statements above, we can get some mixed messages about needing help. Thanks to social media it is now easier than ever to get the mistaken impression that everyone else seems to be "doing just fine."

Getting better at asking for help. If you have never asked for help before, or tried to ask for help, but did not get your needs met, it may be that you could use some assistance asking for help. Consider the following guidelines:

Ask the right person/people/organization. If you go to a bakery looking for tools to build a box, say a hammer and nails, you will probably end up being frustrated. This seems obvious, but our actions might be just as pointless when we go to the wrong source for assistance. We ask a family member who we know has limits to try to fulfill a need beyond their means. We ask a friend or romantic partner to support us in a way that is not within their emotional capability. Have you been shopping for a hammer in a bakery? It might be time to go to the hardware store.

Consider your options/do some research. Let's say you are struggling to pay your bills, or battling with a habit that is getting in the way your happiness, or perhaps on-line dating is not working for you. There are two ways you can conduct research: Ask a trusted friend or mentor, or conduct an online search. Each option is valid. Asking a friend or mentor gives you the benefit of getting a vetted referral to an expert. An online search allows you to find help in a more discrete way. Check out the list of resources in Appendix A to get started.

Give back. If you are still feeling resistant about asking for help, know that this resistance is normal. Most emerging adults are working to establish independence and will feel ambivalent, even resentful toward those that are helping them. Consider the following cognitive shifts:

- I may need some help now, but once I'm on more solid ground, I can take what I've learned and help others.
- Reaching out for help gives me the opportunity to meet new people.
- Each time I search for help, I get better at finding the right resource.
- I will practice gratitude, even though I'm a little resistant to it. I'm aware of the research that confirms that practicing gratitude is good for my health and well-being.*

*See the *Center Points* exercise "Taking a Gratitude Break" in Chapter 7.

Mindful Communication Often Requires Follow-up

Goals:
- Staying grounded during tough conversations
- Repairing relationships after miscommunication

Exercise:

We need to have a talk: The follow-up conversation.

Feeling misunderstood is painful. Are you haunted by a conversation that went poorly? It may seem frightening, but follow-up conversations are an important part of healthy communication. Read these tips then practice with a friend or mentor before having your follow-up conversation.

- **Mindful breathing.** Before having your important conversation, take a few deep diaphragmatic breaths. Review some of the balancing exercises in Chapter 5 so that you can go into the conversation with a calm nervous system.

- **Body awareness/centering.** Scan your body for tension. Are there areas in your body that feel painful and tense? It is common to feel constriction in the stomach or the throat before having an important conversation. Breathe into these areas to release tension.

- **What is the purpose of the conversation?** Prepare for your conversation by thinking about or writing down in your centering journal a clear purpose for the conversation. Is it to clear up a misunderstanding, make an apology, or make a request? Being clear about your purpose will help you preserve the relationship and get what you need from the conversation.

- **My identity?** Think about your side of the story, and what the story means to you. Are you afraid of how this situation affects your reputation? When expressing your story, start your sentences with "I" statements, such as, "I feel badly about the way our evening ended last night." The best way to feel good about a conversation is to be authentic and honest about how the situation has affected you.

- **What feelings does the situation invoke?** Contrary to popular belief, being in touch with your feelings will not weaken your message. In fact knowing what buttons are pushed in the situation will help you stay in control of your emotions as opposed to being swept up by them. Wise decision-making uses both sides of the brain, both logic and emotion.

- **Their identity?** Think about the other person's side of the story. Having a sense of the other person's point of view might help you find a good place to start the conversation.

- **What might they be feeling?** What emotions might the situation be eliciting in the other person? Can you feel compassion for their point of view?

- **Is there common ground?** Is there another story – one that combines a solution that meets everyone's needs?

- **View the situation with a beginners mind.** Even if this is a conversation you have had many times, there may be new information. Use the mindfulness attitude of beginners mind when listening to the other side of the story. Beginners mind requires that you see a person or situation with no preconceived notions. This will stop you from jumping to conclusions, and help the other party feel deeply heard.

- **After going through these steps, do you still want to have this conversation?** Postponing the conversation is sometimes the best option. You may decide at this time that you want to clear your head with some of the *Center Points* exercises found in Chapters 5 or 7. Oftentimes insight and answers to problems are found in moments of mindfulness.

- **Does this situation require more than one follow-up conversation?** If you decide to go through with the conversation, take some time to evaluate what you learned from the situation after the fact. Assertive communication honors all parties involved and takes patience and courage. It also takes practice. Remember that communication is an ongoing process and situations require a few rounds of negotiation.

Self-Compassion 101:
Why self-compassion will help you connect with others

Goals:
- Exploring the research on self-compassion
- Understanding the difference between self-compassion and self-esteem
- Using an analogy to picture wrapping yourself in self-compassion

Self-compassion, the practice of extending kindness inward toward the self, might seem self-indulgent. But self-compassion is actually an important life skill that helps us connect with others and bounce back from failure. Research conducted by Dr. Kristin Neff shows that self-compassion even helps with creativity and motivation and improves mental health. Remember the research and read on!

Self-compassion vs. self-esteem

Self-compassion asks us to honor ourselves whether we are experiencing success or failure. Self-esteem, on the other hand, requires a positive self-evaluation, usually contingent upon reaching certain external goals. Self-compassion is less contingent on outside factors.

Keep these components of self-compassion in mind
- Self-compassion is not selfish. In fact, the more we can offer self-compassion toward ourselves, the more we are able to be compassionate toward others.
- Self-compassion connects us to others. The more we can be accepting of our own human imperfection, the more we can connect with others.
- Self-compassion improves motivation. When we are too self-critical we throw our nervous system into fight or flight mode, shutting off the flow of ideas in favor of survival.

157

Exercise:

Build a self-compassion sandwich. Wrap yourself in two delicious slices of self-compassion:

- For the first slice: Start the day with five minutes of self-compassion. Before you go to sleep tonight, leave pen and paper next to your bed. As you wake up, notice the thoughts that enter your mind. Scan for negativity. Are you reviewing yesterday's failures? Judging yourself harshly as you get dressed? This is an opportunity to practice self-compassion. Put a hand on your heart, and come up with a sentence or phrase that you would say to a good friend. Here are some examples: You don't have to be stressed out all the time to be living a good life. You don't have to beat yourself up. It doesn't help you accomplish your goals anyway. You can make mistakes and still be valuable. Just like everyone else, you are doing your best.

- Remember the research! Self-compassion will help you stay creative and productive as you go about your day! During the day extend compassion to others. Use the phrase, Just like me. Examples: Just like me, this person wants to feel at peace. Just like me, this person wants to belong.

- And now for the second slice: At the end of the day, take note of what you accomplished. Remembering the research on self-compassion to stay motivated. Knowing that it not only improves mental health, but will help you reach your goals, how can you wind down your day in a gentle way? Do something that is completely restorative, or perhaps make a list of three accomplishments.

Practice the self-compassion sandwich for 40 days. Jot down the changes in your stress level in your centering journal to keep track of your progress and note the effect self-compassion has on your mood and productivity.

Intensity Versus Intimacy in a Romantic Relationship

Goals:
- Gaining clarification between deep connection and passing infatuation
- Maximizing enjoyment and minimizing the downside of dating

The beginnings of an intense romantic relationship can be exciting and fun. Being clear about the difference between intensity and intimacy, and knowing what you want from a relationship can help you stay balanced and avoid disappointment.

Exercise:

Studies show that falling in love activates areas of the brain associated with gut feelings and euphoria. The frontal lobe area, associated with higher thought, is not especially active. So how do you keep your feet on the ground when you are attracted to someone?

Answer these questions to help boost your intimacy IQ.

Intimacy involves closeness, comfort, familiarity, trust, and acceptance.
- Can I talk openly to my partner about my fears?
- Can I talk openly to my partner about my hopes and dreams?
- Can I talk openly to my partner about my past?
- Can I accept my partner's past?
- Can I listen and support my partner in conversations about fears, hopes, and dreams?
- Do I feel safe with my partner?

If you answered yes to most of these questions, you are on your way to establishing intimacy.

Intensity usually involves feelings of euphoria and preoccupation.

- We have been physically close, but I really don't know much about my new partner.
- My partner doesn't really seem to be interested in things that are important to me.
- There has been a lot of "love bombing" – Heavy doses of romantic gestures and flattery, but not a lot of authenticity.
- Does my partner try to change me?
- Do I try to change my partner?
- Does my partner often disappoint me by changing plans or otherwise being inconsistent?

If you agree with or answer yes to most of the above statements, you may be in the throws of an intense romantic and physical relationship. There may be nothing wrong with this! Just make sure that you are on the same page about the direction of the relationship.

Mindfulness for a Broken Heart

Goals:
- Normalizing and surviving the difficult but universal emotions of grief and loss
- Writing a recovery plan

Exercise:

You are not alone! If you have recently experienced the loss of a love, mindfulness can help you through the healing process. Here are just a few suggestions to help you on your road to feeling whole again.

- **The pain of a broken heart may come in waves** – You may feel intense feelings of grief over the next few days and weeks. Know that these feelings are a normal part of the healing process. Think of them as a bitter medicine that you must take in small doses to feel better. Watch as the waves of sadness, shock, anger, shame, and feelings of rejection rise, have a peak, and then disappear. Trust in the fact that this is a form of healing, and these emotions have a beginning, middle, and end. Notice the peace and stillness that comes after they pass. Practicing a series of long slow inhales, followed by slightly longer exhales will help calm your nervous system as you work through these waves. Devise your own stress reduction plan using the tools in Chapter 5. In your centering journal write an action statement about your plan.

- **Treat yourself like you have the flu** – There's a physiological reason you may feel like you were punched in the gut. Did you know that the area in the brain that is active when we are experiencing physical pain overlaps with the area that is active when we experience social

161

rejection? Attend to the physical manifestations of a broken heart by taking long walks, or start a totally new exercise routine. It is important to balance your waves of pain with some healthy distractions like exercise, moderate amounts of sleep, and a healthy diet. Take some time to outline a new but gentle physical routine for the first few weeks of healing.

- **Don't isolate yourself** – The temptation to hide in your room might be strong, especially if you and your ex-beloved shared the same group of friends. Make attempts at connecting with new people. If you are in school, consider joining a new club. Explore community projects that might need your help. Helping others who are in need will restore your sense of self-worth. Building compassion for yourself as well as others is at the heart of mindfulness and healing. Think of three ways you can connect with others to avoid isolation. Write them in your centering journal.

- **Don't self-medicate** – Healing requires taking scheduled breaks in the day to monitor your breathing and your thoughts and these breaks will prevent your break-up from becoming a full-blown downward spiral. By coming back to the breath and the body in an intentional way several times throughout the day, you can be curious about any destructive cravings you may have, instead of giving into them. What go-to unhealthy behaviors do you want to try to avoid while you heal?

- **Limit your social media use** – If you see pictures of the one you long to see every time you go on social media, this will prolong your pain. Consider limiting your social media use. Use a phone, email, or voicemail to make plans with friends. What would help you avoid social media during this time?

- **What was missing?** – As you start to heal from your break-up you may start to see that you were not getting all your needs met in the relationship. Now is a good time to take a look at your values and deeply held desires. What is it that you hold most important in your life? What steps can you take to incorporate your values in your life in an intentional way? Set a timer for five minutes. Focus only on your breath, and grab your centering journal and free-write about where you want to be in one year.

- **You are not alone!** – One of the great outcomes of mindfulness is growth in the understanding that we are all connected – that we are not so different from everyone else. Heartache is part of the human condition and none of us is immune to this fact. Mindfulness reminds us that this condition is temporary. Stay connected with family, good friends, or mentors who can help you heal your heart and reconnect with your true self. What aspects of your true self were put on the back burner during your relationship? What activities do you want to try that reflect your true nature?

- **What have you learned from your journey?** – Mindfulness helps us learn from our mistakes. Trust in the fact that mindfulness engages the more rational side of the brain, helping you to move forward with clear intention. How will you use mindfulness to heal your heart? (Some examples: Gentle yoga, guided relaxation, bringing your thoughts back to the present.) Another good way to solidify a lesson is to share your hard-won wisdom with a good friend who is experiencing a broken heart. Listening to another's pain is an act of compassion and will help you to continue to heal.

163

Visualization to Help Calm Social Anxiety

Goals:
- Identifying distorted thoughts that get in the way of deep connections with others
- Using mindfulness as a tool to tame and reframe distorted thoughts

Social anxiety is a common but frustrating problem. The following exercise uses Mindfulness-based Cognitive-Behavioral techniques to help you build up a center of calm and prepare you for the next anxiety-provoking social engagement.

Exercise:

Try the following visualization after 10 to 20 minutes of mindfulness meditation or another calming and centering exercise like gentle stretching.

- During your mindfulness practice, pay particular attention to any negative thoughts you have. Practice detaching from these thoughts by repeating a phrase like, I don't have to react to these thoughts, or I'm working on changing these thoughts.

- Work through the following visualization to get a better idea of how and when feelings of social shyness emerge. It may be helpful to have a mentor read the following paragraph as you close your eyes and visualize the situation. Finally, use this visualization to reframe a real situation that has occurred in your own life.

Take a few deep breaths and visualize a social situation that makes you mildly to moderately uncomfortable. Do not use a situation that causes full-blown panic for this exercise. Let's use the example of attending a party with your partner, or a friend that you feel very comfortable with. Picture the room where the party is being held in detail. Using all your senses, picture the lights and sounds. Is there music playing, are people laughing and talking? Can you smell food? Visualize yourself coming into the party with your friend or partner. What thoughts are going through your mind? Are your thoughts about yourself unkind? Take a moment to list them in your centering journal.

- What physical symptoms of social anxiety does this scene evoke? Take a breath, scan your body, and list your physical symptoms.

- What unproductive behaviors (behaviors that will not help you reduce your anxiety the next time you find yourself at a party) might you engage in?

- As you picture yourself slipping into a social behavior pattern that keeps you stuck in anxiety, imagine that you remember mindfulness. You remember that you can take a deep breath, release the tension in your body, challenge your negative thoughts, and extend loving kindness to yourself and others. You remember that others in the room may also feel anxious. You feel safe in this social situation and connected to others.

With practice, this mindfulness exercise can help you tame social anxiety even in high-stress situations.

Switch from Comparing to Connecting

Goals:
- Building awareness of comparing yourself to others and the negative emotions that follow
- Decreasing judgmental thoughts and building equanimity
- Increasing happiness for others to decrease jealousy and envy (sympathetic joy)

Comparison is the thief of joy.

— Theodore Roosevelt

Can you relate to Theodore Roosevelt's famous quote?

Comparing and categorizing is big part of how we make it through the day. This skill helps us save time and feel less overwhelmed in new situations. However, overuse of this mostly unconscious process can feed anxiety and feelings of being less than others or better than others that lead to separation, isolation, and in extreme cases, to exclusion and violence.

Taking a nonjudgmental stance, both toward others and ourselves is one of the cornerstones of mindfulness. This ability to step back and detach (applying equanimity) is a skill that will decrease anxiety, stress, and discontent and increase feelings of connection to the human race. Additionally, practicing happiness for others' good fortune (sympathetic joy) can also increase connection.

Taking a nonjudgmental stance is easier said than done, as we humans are so good at judging. Our primitive nervous system tricks us into believing that by sizing up and categorizing people, places, and things we will keep ourselves safe from harm.

While using good judgment can certainly keep us safe from harm, excessive judgment that deems us as better than or less than creates an artificial wall.

Exercise:

Try this mindfulness experiment on your next walk, trip to a grocery store, or other task that puts you in the midst of people that you do not know.

Start by taking a few deep breaths, which will help you calm your nervous system and take a neutral stance.

As you walk down the road or the grocery aisle, note the thoughts that pop into your head. You might mentally register someone as short, tall, bald, smarter than me, better dressed than me, or poorer than me.

Resist this urge to go on autopilot by thoughtlessly labeling your subject. Instead of using one or two descriptive words, try using the phrase "Just like me" as you make your observations. Here are a few examples:

- Just like me, this person looks tired.
- Just like me, this person may be worried.
- Just like me, this person can feel joy.
- Just like me, this person wants to be loved.

If you see a person who seems happy – a small child playing, laughing friends, a couple holding hands – practice feeling joy for the presence of this happiness in the world. If you feel envious, try repeating the following phrases to yourself:

- This person's happiness helps balance out the worlds suffering.
- There is enough happiness in the world for both you and me.
- Your happiness is my happiness.

See if this mindfulness experiment helps you to feel less critical, more joyful, and more connected to the condition we call being human. When you get home, write about it in your centering journal.

Fear of Missing Out (FOMO):
And other ways of feeling left behind

Goals:
- Normalizing the human tendency to worry about being left out
- Appreciating where you are, not where you want to be
- Creating a FOMO action plan

Exercise:

If you are feeling disappointed, maybe even envious, because of a missed opportunity, it is a good time to apply mindfulness. Here are three tips that can help you feel like you are in the right place at the right time.

Name your emotion – know the science. Saying quietly to yourself or a trusted friend, I am disappointed, or I am jealous, or I am frustrated can help you register in your mind and your body that these feelings are temporary. By verbalizing your emotions you will be activating left-brain activity that helps you put a logical spin on the situation.

Consider that conditions may not be right. Noting that now may not be the best time for the change you desire may stop you from blaming yourself and help find an alternative activity with self-compassion.

Clear your mind. When things don't go the way we plan, we tend to obsess about what went wrong. Take five minutes to focus on the breath gently bringing your thoughts back if they stray. Remember that your mindfulness practice will boost your ability to gain insight into any situation, promoting a sense of calm and well-being, even in imperfect times.

What is the next best thing to do? Sitting at home on a weekend night and waiting for a call back for a second date can really put your self-esteem and mood in a tailspin. Sometimes deep breathing isn't enough, and mindful action is what is called for. Ask yourself what is the best thing to do in this moment? The key to feeling better in FOMO situations usually does NOT entail spending time on Facebook. Instead, call a friend or do something solo that has brought you joy in the past. Watch out for the isolation spiral. Make an action plan to be around friends, new or old, within the next 48 hours.

Write a FOMO action plan statement in your centering journal. Include three easy to implement steps. See the example below:

1. *The next time I feel left out I will call a trusted friend or family member who will understand my reaction to the situation.*
2. *The next time I feel that I am missing out on a social situation I will start by going for a fast walk. I know that ten minutes outside always clears my head.*
3. *The next time I'm worried about missing out I will look for an alternative activity that I can invite a friend to, or attend solo. I will stay off of social media that might increase my feelings of FOMO and set a goal to meet up with close friends within 24 hours.*

Getting Ready for Your Work Evaluation

Goals:
- Understanding the dynamics of a work evaluation
- Practicing three skills that will help you feel good after the evaluation

In the first few years of your work life the thought of sitting down with a supervisor for a work evaluation can be terrifying. I have listened to many stories of the anxiety that this process elicits. One young person I know said she automatically started crying when she so much as thought about her upcoming job evaluation. There's a better way to prepare.

Exercise:

Consider the following tips. Practice at least three before your review.

Know the process: You probably already have a sense of your supervisor's style. But if you don't, make sure to ask a more experienced mentor. Ask your supervisor directly for the details of the evaluation process. The more armed you are with facts the less room there will be to make up horror stories in your head. Here are some appropriate ways to ask:
- I'm new to this process; can you explain to me how this review will work?
- I haven't been through this process at this company yet. Can you let me know what to expect?

Know your audience: Once you know your supervisor's style, dance with it! Take a trick from mindfulness theory and stay curious about any feedback by asking follow up questions. Don't take feedback personally. Consider that your manager's style has nothing to do with you.

Know your HR policies: Being familiar with your organization's human resource policies can buy you some time if you get thrown a curve ball during the review.

Consider this a chance to improve relationships: Instead of feeling like you are in front of a firing squad, take this opportunity to improve relationships. Ask your supervisor questions about the vision for the organization. If appropriate, ask about their career path or their experience as a young adult in the workplace.

Ask for time: "May I have time to think about your comments?" If you receive unexpected feedback about improvement, listen to the suggestions given to you with respect. Remember: Don't take it personally, take it under consideration instead. Do take the opportunity to ask for time to think about the review and schedule a follow-up.

Pull in your values inventory* and remember your strengths: Towards the end of the review, wear the hat of a consumer. Now that you are clear about what the organization expects from you, think about what you want from the organization. This does not mean asking for a big pay increase (although in some instances, this might be appropriate). This is a good time to ask about training that might expand your job skills.

Reward yourself: Phew! Aren't you glad that's over with? Reward yourself for making it through this rite of passage! What did you learn from the experience? List three skills that you want to practice in your next evaluation. (Example: being more assertive about asking for a raise or a change in schedule). Record them in your centering journal. You will want to re-read it before next year's evaluation.

* A values inventory can be found in Chapter 8.

Summary:

The emerging adult years are filled with important social firsts like interviewing for a full time professional job, navigating your first serious relationship, renting an apartment, or negotiating a raise. Feeling like a fish out-of-water is normal in new situations, even for more experienced adults. Using mindfulness-informed skills, like self-compassion, practicing visualizations before an important event, and quieting self-critical thoughts will help you feel like you are swimming with the current instead of against it. Since we are interconnected, social beings, asking for help is a lifelong practice. Cultivating mindfulness skills through the exercises in this chapter help us stay calm in social situations. Choose one exercise to practice regularly over the next month and improve your relationships with co-workers, friends, and romantic partners.

CHAPTER 7

Focus

Harnessing the powers of concentration

The focus exercises that follow include mindfulness-informed tools designed to increase mental concentration and inner calm. The art and science of focusing has many faces. It may look like a man sitting in solitude on a meditation cushion, or a woman sitting in a café slowly sipping from a paper cup, mindfully watching her thoughts. At other times the face of focus is a person absorbed in an art project, or a group of friends on a ten-mile run, or a teen absorbed in her favorite music. Of course, all of these activities can be done unmindfully – without focus – but they are infinitely more rewarding when performed with attention to the present moment. When we focus on our present moment experience, the brain rewires itself in such a way that it makes the experience more satisfying. With practice, we can gain the ability to focus on demand. Take a minute to think of an area in your life that could benefit from more focus.

Recall Jake's struggle as he decides whether he should stay in his current relationship, and how our session outside of the office helped him to calm down and focus. This example illustrates that focus can arise when we are moving just as easily as when we are sitting. Stilling the mind is what matters. If you are feeling especially physically or mentally agitated, start with the movement exercises offered in this chapter.

Alternatively, if the busyness of your life is getting you down, start with one of the exercises that call for stillness or internal focus. Wherever you start, building mental focus will benefit each one of the four domains of your life.

Center Points on Balance

These are the Center Points exercises you will find in this chapter.

- Focusing Basics for the Severely Distracted
- Respond, Don't React
- Musical Mindfulness
- Take a Gratitude Break
- Collecting Gold – Notice what is going well in your life right now
- Balancing Logic and Intuition
- Where Are You Putting Your Focus
- Raise Your Gaze
- How to Set Yourself up for a Day of Silence
- With Every New Experience – Affirmations to build confidence

Focusing Basics for the Severely Distracted

But it sometimes happens that I cannot easily shake off the village. The thought of some work will run in my head and I am not where my body is, I am out of my senses. In my walks I would fain return to my senses. What business have I in the woods, if I am thinking of something out of the woods?

— Henry David Thoreau

Goals:
- Taking a look at small and easy ways to build focus
- Rating exercises from most to least accessible/doable in your daily life

Starting a meditation practice is a great idea especially with all the research that shows the mental and physical benefits it can bring. But there are times in life (usually when we most need it) when sitting still and calming the mind can seem like a feat of Olympic proportions.

Exercise:

Here are some ideas to find moments of tranquility, even in the most hectic of times. Read through each exercise, then rate them by assigning three stars to the exercise you would be most likely to try today, two stars to an exercise you are willing to try tomorrow, and one star to an exercise you can commit to trying by the end of the week. Commit to completing a three star exercise today.

Take note of what is distracting you – If you don't feel ready for a meditation practice it's okay. Start by noticing what is distracting you.

- Are your distractions fear-based – are you worrying about some future outcome?
- Are your distractions fantasy-based – is there something you don't have that is stopping you from living your life in the here and now?
- Start by noting what takes you out of the present moment – just taking note of what is keeping you in a state of distraction is a step toward mindfulness.

Perform a single routine task mindfully – fold laundry, wash dishes, feed the dog without slipping into autopilot. So often, we get up in the morning and do our routine in zombie mode.

- Get out of bed and stretch for half a minute.
- What is the first thing you usually do in the morning? Can you do it with all your senses engaged?
- Resist automatic thoughts and mentally rehearsing your to-do list.
- You might find that the routine task is actually enjoyable, or you may decide to change the start of your day so that the very first task is something that feels pleasant, like reading a few pages in a good book versus checking your email.

Take a slow walk or run – Routine exercise is another place where we can easily check our focus.

- Take your walk or go to the gym as usual, but consciously slow down your pace.
- Notice something new about the gym or the walking/running route you are on.
- Refrain from projecting into the future or thinking about the past. Sure, you may burn a few less calories by slowing down, but what you gain in tranquility and calm will more than make up for it.

Pet or play with an animal – If you have one, your dog or cat can become your Zen master.

- Take time out today to be with your pet and just with your pet. Animals are experts in being in the present moment.
- Get down on the floor and get on your pet's level. Gaze into their eyes as you play with or pet them.
- Thank them for being your Zen master.

Belly breathe with a baby or small child – Babies and young children can also anchor us to the present moment in a special way.

- If you have an infant in your life, take some time to watch them while they nap. Babies have not learned the bad habit of taking shallow breaths. Take long, slow breaths like a baby.
- If you have a toddler in your life, ask him or her to lie on the floor next to you. Place pillows on your bellies. Watch them as they float up and down on your belly as you take long, deep inhales and exhales.
- Take some time to giggle with your toddler as the pillows rise and fall.

Walk barefoot – If the temperature allows, kick your shoes off and walk in the grass for a few minutes.

- Walking barefoot requires mindfulness to avoid sharp objects or other outdoor goop.
- It is also immensely grounding and healing.
- Focus on how it feels to connect directly with the earth.

Meet your energy level with self-compassion. If you are low on energy, or going through a stressful time, it can be counter-productive to try to force yourself to concentrate harder. Use the above suggestions to anchor yourself in the present moment in small doses that will add up to improved mood and concentration. By practicing small doses of mindful focus, the fog will lift and you will feel more energized.

Which exercise can you commit to today? Choose a few of the focusing exercises that seem most accessible to you. Write a plan stating how and when you will try the exercises. Journal about them in your centering journal.

Respond, Don't React

Between stimulus and response there is a space.
In that space is our power to choose our response.
In our responses lies our growth, and or freedom.

— Attributed to Victor Frankl

Goals:
- Exploring the consequences of reacting versus responding
- Building your capacity to react in a thoughtful manner

Oh…the dreaded anger hangover, the words or actions we can't undo…. We've all been there. Maybe it was a simple instance of road rage, or an outburst of frustration directed toward a roommate, leaving you with an emotional mess to clean up. Even worse is the thoughtless word or action directed toward someone we love. These outbursts are hard on everyone.

Exercise:

One of the great benefits of mindfulness practice is that it helps us build space between thought, word, and action. This increases the frequency of thoughtful responses that leave no harm in their wake, and decreases the number of actions we regret. When we thoughtfully respond we are taking all sides of the situation into account, fostering responses based on compassion and personal values, as opposed to fear or anger. The following tips will help you increase the gaps between thought, word, and action.

- **Know your triggers:** If you are going to be around people that tend to trigger negative reactions from you, whether in a social or work setting; be prepared. Before that contentious work meeting, practice the suggestions in the exercise entitled "Breathing for Balance" in Chapter 5.

- **What if I wait?** You are out with several friends, including one "frenemy." Your frenemy brings up the subject of your ex-boyfriend and his upcoming wedding. You are certain this comment was meant to get a rise out of you, and you are tempted to respond with some sharp sarcasm, maybe pointing out the fact that your frenemy hasn't been on a date in over six months. What if you wait? Instead, ask yourself, "Is this reaction anger-based or fear-based?" If the answer is yes to either of these questions, it may be wise to wait.

- **Do I want to be right…or do I want to be happy, kind, accepting?** This is always a good question to ask before any verbal response. Chances are, other people around you, at least the more mindful people, already registered your frenemy's comment as slightly unkind. Drop the temptation to turn conversations into power plays. When given the choice between being right and being kind, chose kind. Then you will always be right.

- **How do I want to feel when I wake up tomorrow?** When we feel angry or threatened by someone's comments or behavior, the rational part of our brain, the wise and cautious pre-frontal cortex, goes off-line and the defensive, reactive, fight-or-flight brain takes over. This more primitive part of the brain deceives us, telling us that if we attack and conquer, the situation will be over and we will have won. But anyone who has lost their cool and then felt regret the next day knows that reactivity usually leads to more suffering, and it is most often ours.

- **H.A.L.T!:** Take a lesson from the 12-step recovery community. Remember the acronym H.A.L.T. Are you feeling Hungry, Angry, Lonely, or Tired? Anyone of these physiological/emotional states can lead to unskillful reactivity and inappropriate responses.

- **Employ beginners mind, not a here we go again mind:** The best example to illustrate this tip is to think about what it is like to go home and visit family. We can spend the journey home anticipating the frustrating behavior of a relative that gets under our skin. Or, we can keep an open mind, an open heart, and act as if we are just getting to know our well-known relative. If a relative makes a hurtful comment, use phrases such as, "What do you mean?" and "I hear you say…" It gives the speaker a chance to explain, or it gives the questioner who was offended by the comment a chance to take a few deep breaths.

- **Freedom, Freedom, Freedom!:** Chant "freedom, freedom, freedom!" to yourself over and over, remembering the freedom that comes from NOT reacting, from not boxing yourself into a corner verbally.

- **Rehearse:** After reading each tip, ask a mentor or a friend to role-play a situation that might be potentially triggering a situation. Rehearsing helps you internalize new skills and uncover possible pitfalls that might arise during an actual interaction. You can also rehearse by noticing how you react in small risk situations, such as reacting calmly if you spill a few drops of water on your shirt.

- **And lastly, think big picture:** What do you want your response to say about you? If you are leading with your values (see Chapter 8) and compassion, will you be able to look back at the situation and feel at peace. A thoughtful response will always foster more internal peace and ease. Learning to be less reactive takes practice. Be gentle with yourself as you learn.

- **Write about your experiences and thoughts in your centering journal.** Remember that journaling is not writing an essay. Jot down your thoughts without undue concern about form, grammar, or spelling.

Musical Mindfulness

Goal:
- Exploring practices that help you use music as a mindfulness tool

One of the wonderful qualities of mindful focus is that it is accessible to everyone, no matter what learning style you favor. If you are musically inclined, let your mindfulness practice be lyrical. Music and dance can be a great object of concentration. Think of the Whirling Dervishes of Turkey who combine music, dance, and devotion to reach an intense state of concentration and connection. Picture a jazz band starting out on stage with a scripted piece of music, and then finding such concentration and connection that they make new and beautiful music on the spot. Imagine you are a dancer, completing the perfect grand jeté to your favorite music.

Exercise:

Build a meditative relationship with music. Use the following tips to get started.

- You can use any kind of music to support your practice. Keep in mind that when you're meditating, you are aiming for a calm and alert state of mind. When using music to meditate, it's important to choose music that will relax you, but not put you to sleep. True meditation requires that you stay awake. The brain waves of a sleeping person and that of a meditating person are much different.

- Try to strike a balance with music that is soothing and gentle, but will not have you snoring. Many classical pieces are appropriate for attaining this middle ground of a calm and alert mind, as are many modern pieces.

- Traditional chants and chimes are also a good choice when experimenting with musical meditation. Chanting and chimes or bells have been used for centuries by many different cultures to induce a meditative state. It may take some experimenting to find a recording that is right for you.

- A piece of music you have always loved might be just right when you are starting out with music meditation. If you are listening to an old favorite, consider listening to the music with beginner's mind – a term used by mindfulness meditation practitioners that describes approaching an experience with a fresh perspective. Listen to the piece as if it's the first time you ever heard it, focusing in on the beat of a drum, or the tone of a violin. Listening to music in this way will put you in a true meditative state.

- You'll know you are in a meditative state when you find yourself relaxed and yet mentally engaged with the piece of music to which you are listening. Distractions fall into the background of your awarenss. With regular practice, meditating with music can help you experience expanded periods of calm and increased concentration.

- You can purchase CD's or download music written specifically for meditation. They are written with a lack of melodic line so that you can concentrate on meditation rather than on what comes next.

- If you use music you have loved for years you will need to work hard not to associate it with events of the past, good or bad. This will interfere with your current meditation. For example: Listening to Yo-Yo Ma's cello solos take me back to watching my very talented sister perform the same pieces. I might have a lovely time thinking of her, but I am not meditating as I had planned.

- Create a meditation track of your own with tunes that have helped you in the past. If you have a handful of special songs or music scores that have always helped you feel calm, put them together on one CD or playlist.

Two things to watch out for:

- Avoid music that makes you excessively sad. We all love a good breakup song, but the goal of this exercise is to enjoy the sounds and melodies of the music, and foster a neutral mood.
- If your meditation music really puts you in the zone, do not use it when you are driving.

Take a Gratitude Break

Goals:
- Understanding the benefits of gratitude
- Looking at why gratitude may be difficult for emerging adults
- Building a small and sustainable gratitude practice

There is a growing body of evidence that shows that practicing gratitude can lift your mood, increase your level of contentment and even improve your physical health. But how do you get started – and what if you don't feel grateful about anything?

Gratitude conflict

For emerging adults, gratitude can be especially tricky. When you are trying to establish independence you might feel a mixture of gratitude and something like resentment toward those upon whom you are dependent. The push and pull between independence and gratitude can cause feelings of guilt to arise. Instead of focusing on guilt, accept gratitude conflict as part of your striving for independence. If gratitude toward those you are dependent on is difficult right now, focus on other areas of life where you do feel grateful.

Exercise:

Read the following scientific tidbits that show the health benefits of gratitude:

- Adults who keep gratitude journals exercise more regularly, have fewer physical complaints, and feel better and more optimistic about their future.

187

- When people focus on gratitude they feel more loving, forgiving, and enthusiastic.

- Practicing gratitude can help raise your happiness set-point – Positive psychology researchers describe the natural temperament range that we are born with as our happiness "set-point." Mindfulness practices like gratitude help raise our set-point.

- Practicing gratitude fights the natural tendency to have the good feelings of a fortunate experience fade away.

Put gratitude into practice:

- Allocate time every day to look at what is going right in your life. This may be first thing in the morning, or before bed.

- Think small. Maybe you didn't win the lottery today, but did you feel healthy, or enjoy a nice interaction with someone at the bank? Did you happen to notice a tree blossoming? Is there a recent event that you initially saw as a set-back that with some time and distance, you can now feel grateful for experiencing?

- Get a gratitude partner. Find a friend, co-worker, even a child who can help you notice the good things that are happening.

- Share you gratitude. When you are feeling grateful for a person, place, or thing, share your experience with a trusted friend – someone who will be happy that you are happy.

- Journal about how you felt when you verbalized gratitude. Was it uplifting? Did it strengthen your feeling of being loved and appreciated?

Collecting Gold – Notice what is going on in your life right now

Goals:
- Increasing your awareness of positive experiences
- Recording positive experiences to help counter the brain's negativity bias – the brain's natural tendency to focus on the negative.

In the previous exercise, you were asked to cultivate feelings of gratitude. We also acknowledged that there are periods in life where gratitude feels out of reach. The negativity bias is the mind's natural tendency to focus on what is going wrong, what is missing, or out of place. This negativity bias often keeps us safe. An obvious example would be walking down the street and seeing a sparking electric wire that has been dislodged from a pole after a storm. The negativity bias helps tell us, "Something is out of place and may be dangerous." To keep from noticing negativity all day, every day, we can collect gold by noticing what is going right in life.

A Step Toward More Positive Emotions: Mindfulness-based cognitive therapy

In mindfulness-based cognitive therapy, individuals are encouraged to take note of what is going right.

Keeping a record of positive events can help counter our natural tendency to scan our environment for what is going wrong.

Exercise:

Keep a record of positive events. This exercise encourages us to spend more time thinking about pleasant events and consequently feeling the pleasant emotions that go with the event. This is not about reliving monumental joyous events, but rather noticing the

189

small moments of daily pleasure that we often overlook. Here are the steps to recording pleasant events, along with examples:

- Record the event – at the end of the day, take note of a small pleasant event that moved your mood in a positive direction, "I had a good conversation with my co-worker today."

- Note pleasant sensations you felt during the event: "We laughed about how crazy it was when we were trying to make the deadline for our boss. That felt much better than complaining."

- Note in detail physical sensations that occurred during the event, "It was a little like a switch was flipped. I felt lighter, less serious, less stuck in my head."

- Note your mood, feelings, and thoughts that accompanied the event, "I definitely felt happier. Before we talked I was feeling like I was the only one who was stressed out. I felt more connected to my co-workers."

- Notice your mood in the present moment while you are remembering and recording the event, "I'm feeling a little better about going to work tomorrow, and a little more positive about the next deadline that is around the corner."

- In this example recording the event helped reduce a sense of worry about upcoming deadlines – negative, stressful emotions, and increased a feeling of shared experience and confidence about upcoming projects – a more positive emotion.

Remember the science: Focusing on pleasant events rewires the brain. Over time the ability to focus on positive experiences will happen more frequently.

Balancing Logic and Intuition

Goals:
- Learning some facts about the left and right hemispheres of your brain
- Harnessing and integrating different brain activities to boost focus, and aid in decision-making

We live in a culture that rewards left-brain logic and mistrusts right-brain intuition. If you have spent the last few years immersed in school or job training, you may have had your intuitive brain trained right out of you! The cultural left-brain bias is starting to shift, and contemplative neuroscience is helping us balance this bias. Brain science is revealing that we need both left-brain logic and right-brain gut feelings to make good decisions.

Left versus right brain

The left-brain is task-focused and logical. It governs linear thought, math calculation, and verbal detail. The left-brain sees the trees, while the right brain sees the forest. Left-brain functioning allows us to read individual words and master small muscular control. The left-brain helps us with routine and sameness.

The right-brain is creative and visionary. It helps us see the big picture, and actually gets involved in solving math problems once the left-brain identifies individual units and numbers. The right-brain sees the forest, and the left brain the trees. Although the left-brain is responsible for verbal detail (the meaning of individual words) the right-brain is responsible for reading (comprehension). The right-brain likes novelty, and newness.

Integration is the key to good decision-making

Integrating our holistic, nonverbal, emotional quotient, or our capability to recognize our own, and other people's emotions – in other words, the big picture – with our logical, detail-oriented intelligence quotient helps us make better decisions based not only on fact, but also on past experience, values, and empathy.

Too much focus on logical processes can make us rigid, and cut off from emotion. On the other hand, too much of a focus on emotional input can lead to chaos.

Genetic factors play a major role in whether we are right- or left-brain dominant. However, contemplative neuroscience shows that mindfulness exercises can help with right/left integration. Meditation, yoga, and other contemplative practices strengthen an area in the mid-brain called the insula. The insula helps us connect and integrate facts with gut feeling, emotions with logic.

Try these left/right-balancing exercises to help with integration:

- **Name it to tame it:** The next time you are feeling ruled by emotion try verbally stating the emotion out loud. Announcing, "I'm feeling anxious about my date tonight." even to yourself, takes the right-brain emotion and moves it to a left-brain fact. This is one of the reasons talking with friends or a therapist calms the nervous system.

- **Crossing over:** Any physical activity that encourages you to coordinate the left and right side of the body helps integrate brain activity. The cross over doesn't have to be exaggerated. Going for a walk and swinging your arms will do the trick. If you can't get outside, stand up and march in place. Tap your left knee with your right hand and your right knee with your left hand.

192

- **Yogic breathing:** There are many Pranayamas that integrate and balance the right and left side of the brain. Try this simple technique:
  * Stand with your feet hip-width apart, knees slightly bent
  * Bend your arms as if you are flexing your biceps and place your fingertips lightly on the very top of your shoulders
  * Make sure your shoulders are relaxed and not tensed up toward your ears
  * Inhale, filling your lungs halfway as you twist from your waist through the crown of your head to the left, complete the inhale as you twist to right
  * Exhale halfway and punch your right fist in front of you, complete then exhale as you punch your left fist forward
  * Repeat 6-10 times
  * Return to a natural breathing rhythm and notice change in your clarity

- **Use your non-dominant hand:** The next time you find yourself having difficulty making a decision, use your non-dominant hand. If you are right handed write a few sentences, doodle, or color with your left hand. Take twenty minutes to go back and forth between your dominant and non-dominant hands.

Where Are You Putting Your Focus?

Goal:
  * Becoming more aware of how technology, socializing, and solitude affect your mood and ability to focus

Because of our culture's heavy use of technology let's consider three major points of focus: On our internal experience, on others, and on technology. Each area of focus can be the cause of satisfaction or discomfort.

Point of Focus	Satisfaction	Dissatisfaction
Focus on self	Hanging out alone helps me de-stress. I like having a little me time.	I haven't talked to my friends all weekend. I'm feeling kind of anxious and lonely.
Focus on others	It's so great to be enjoying this concert with friends.	I haven't had a second to myself all week.
Focus on technology	It was fun and relaxing to play video games today.	I spent three hours on Facebook this afternoon comparing my summer with my roommate's. She definitely has a better social life than I do.

Exercise:

Consider the chart above and think about your relationship with each point of focus. We all need to strike a balance with the three points. If you feel stuck in an area of unhappy focus, it may be time to switch to another.

Take a piece of paper and some colored pens or pencils. Set a timer for five minutes and free-write or draw about each area of focus. What is your level of satisfaction with each area? If you are feeling dissatisfied, how can you use mindfulness to move toward satisfaction?

Shift Your Perspective

Goals:
- Increasing mental flexibility
- Changing your perspective

You may be starting to see a trend in this chapter – flexibility is a key component in building focus and a healthy brain. When we feel stuck, it is helpful to switch between opposing objects of attention, like big and small, light and dark, far and near. This next exercise helps with changing perspective.

Exercise:

In a world where we spend a good deal of time working on screens, we can become nearsighted not only in our eyes, but in our attitudes. It might be time to shift your gaze. Here's how:

- Close your eyes and take a few deep even breaths, making your exhale slightly longer than your inhale.

- This exercise works best if you are sitting comfortably with a tall spine, and you have access to a window. Being outside is ideal. If you have neither a window nor immediate access to the outside you can use the section of a wall or ceiling that is furthest away from you.

- After taking a few deep breaths, bring your hands in front of your eyes and gently cup your palms over your closed eyes. Take few more breaths.

- Drop your palms, open your eyes, and raise your gaze to the horizon or, for those indoors, to where the wall and ceiling meet.

195

- Let your gaze be soft. Let your thoughts be soft as well.

- Research shows that gazing upward activates areas in the brain that are used during meditation, religious devotion, and creative activities that encourage us to contemplate larger universal connections. After spending some time gazing at the horizon, we can return to the present moment refreshed.

How to Set Yourself Up For a Day of Silence

Goal:
- Preparing yourself for a peaceful day of mindfulness-informed restoration

You don't have to spend big bucks to experience the benefits of a retreat. The best retreats can be had right at home. Preparation is the key.

Exercise:

- Plan a day that you think will work best – when you can take a day off from work and responsibilities. Make sure you let family and friends know that you are taking a full day of silence for yourself and that you will be unreachable, unless in an emergency, of course! Maybe pin a little piece of paper to your chest that reads "In loving silence" so that you can point to it if needed.
- Create a sacred space – this can be as simple as a comfortable chair, or a freshly organized corner in a favorite room. Avoid your bed if you think your day of silence might turn into a day of napping.
- Plan simple meals – the day before your retreat, stock up on simple foods. Soups and simple grain dishes with veggies, and warm caffeine-free beverages are good choices. Since you will be moving slower than your usual pace, you may not be as hungry.
- Close your computer, turn off your phone, put away books that might take you out of the present moment, and sit in silence. Try to bring your attention to your breath. Try some of the breathing exercises described in Chapter 5.
- Plan a seated mindfulness meditation early in the day. Refer

to the guided meditation resources in Appendix A. Perhaps try a slightly longer session than you usually take. Write a sentence or two in your journal about your experience.

- Go for a mindful walk around your neighborhood. Try to take everything in as if seeing it for the first time, taking in the color of paint on houses, sounds, smells in the air that may have become unnoticeable to you. Walk slowly. Take your time. If neighbors say hello, give them a smile or wave.

- Practice your favorite yoga routine or create a new one if you feel bored. Take an extra long savasana (rest pose at the end of practice) today by setting yourself up with extra blankets and props to assist your body to relax as deeply as possible.

- Try Yoga Nidra. Yoga Nidra means "yogic sleep." It is a form of meditation where the practitioner is guided through a detailed body scan. The military and other groups are using Yoga Nidra as an aid to heal trauma. It is deeply relaxing to the nervous system. You can find guided Yoga Nidra exercises on YouTube or check out our favorite Yoga Nidra resources in Appendix A.

- Bath time is a great way to relax. Pour in some Epsom salts and a drop or two of lavender oil. This is an easy and inexpensive way for you to absorb important minerals and relax your mind and body.

- Make sure to try another round of seated mindfulness meditation, a mindful walk, or Yoga Nidra before bed.

Write in your journal before you go to sleep. What were the challenges you faced today and how did you handle them? Did you enjoy the silence or was it uncomfortable? What are some improvements you might make on your next day of silence? Write a sentence or two about the benefits of your meditation day. Keep these sentences close by and pull them out when you need a boost of motivation to be mindful. Remember, your centering journal can be on whatever device you are the most comfortable with.

With Every New Experience: Affirmations to build confidence

Goal:
- Using affirmations to increase confidence

To some, positive affirmations have a bad image. They become relegated to the new age, the fringy, and the comedy skit. With all the solid research that proves that our thoughts shape our brain, maybe it's time to take another look at affirmations.

One of the goals of mindfulness is to let thoughts come and go naturally. Affirmations can help you if you are stuck in a negative thought loop during a meditation session or during your day. This can be a lifesaver if you are in transition, adjusting to a new environment, or when learning a new skill, or feeling overwhelmed or doubtful.

Exercise:

Imagine that you just had a conversation with a co-worker and you find yourself replaying the conversation over and over, looking for flaws, and wishing you could get a take-two. This exercise is designed to help you to break apart obsessive thought loops that take up too much space in your mind. Take a few deep breaths and read through the list below. Over the next few days, use the affirmations that resonate with you the most, or write one or two of your own, and put them in your cell phone or on a sticky note on your laptop. Remember to use your strongest learning style. What would be the most helpful way to integrate your affirmations?

- Through self-care, I become more calm and confident.

- When I practice self-care, my energy becomes more balanced.

- With every new experience, I become more aware of my deepest values and my goals become clearer.

- With every new experience, I am able to make better decisions.

- With every new experience, I grow in my ability to understand others.

- With every new experience, I become more patient and understanding.

- With every new experience, I learn to communicate in an authentic way.

- With every new experience, I allow myself room for imperfection.

- With every new experience, I build confidence. This situation is challenging to me right now, but it will not always be.

- With every new experience, I become more aware of the ebb and flow of my cravings and aversions.

- With every new experience I have more genuine confidence and experience less fear.

- With every new experience, I am better able to manage my emotions.

Summary:

Now that you have worked through the exercises on building focus, can you see how this practice will help you make more skillful choices with your daily routine and in relationships? At this point, it might be helpful to quickly go back through the Balance and Belonging exercises and review your favorite mindfulness skills. Just like exercising a muscle, your ability to focus becomes stronger the more you practice. Remember the neurological benefits of practicing focus. Can you see how technology aids in or detracts from clear focus? How will you use your smartphone to help you practice focusing this week? Is there a digital tool or website that takes you out of focus and away from your goals? What was the one most important lesson you learned by going through the focusing exercises? How will you use them this week to build on your ability to create a healthy routine and surround yourself with a healthy community?

CHAPTER 8

Meaning

Exploring personal values to find joy

The exercises in this chapter are not meant to encourage emerging adults to quit their jobs or drop out of school. Rather, they will help emerging adults make wise adjustments to their current path, leading to more contentment and joy, and will inspire others to do the same. The Meaning exercises are designed to help emerging adults find their heart's deepest longing. Until this point in a young adult's life, many activities have been scripted first by family, and later by social circles. Emerging adulthood is one of the best times in life to identify what you value most. When we listen to our hearts, and at the same time take part in a thoughtful exploration of values, the good life becomes attainable.

Think back to Tracey, the high-functioning young adult we met in earlier chapters. Tracey is struggling to find her own authentic path and individual values. Because she is following a somewhat scripted path that does not necessarily align with her values, she has trouble feeling contentment and joy. Her growing anxiety is actually a healthy warning sign, calling her to slow down long enough to find her heart's deepest longing.

Can you name one or two values that you learned from your family? Your friends? Can you identify a value that comes from your inner self? Write about them in your centering journal.

Center Points on Meaning

These are the Center Points exercises you will find in this chapter.

- Identifying Values, Increasing Joy
- Take the Lesson, Leave the Shame
- Making Sense of the Times in Which You Live
- Surfing the Eight Worldly Winds
- Not Getting What You Want: Taking meaning from frustration and disappointment
- The Four Immeasurable Attitudes
- Practicing Reverence
- The Meaning of Loneliness
- The Components of Confidence
- To Pursue or Not to Pursue: When faced with two or more choices
- How to Organize a *Center Points* Book Club

Identifying Values, Increasing Joy

Goals:
- Defining your personal values
- Using your values as guideposts in decision-making

In the early years of adulthood, it's easy to find yourself on a path that was gently, or not so gently, recommended to you by family or mentors. This road is often one that we see friends and family valuing, not one necessarily made up of your own heart's deepest longing. You may have recieved some of the following messages from friends and family:

- Finish school or learn a trade
- Join the service (we're an Army family)
- Get married early
- Don't get married early
- Join the church
- Whatever you do don't join a church

Following the road of ancestors or peers can be the right move, but when it is done without self-exploration, the road can become joyless not only for yourself, but for those in your life. That is why it's so important to take time to explore your personal values. Consider this quote from the Indian text, *The Bhagavad Gita:*

"Better is one's own dharma (calling) lived out imperfectly, than to follow that of another."

Take some time to explore your values. It's never too late to do this exercise. Even if you find yourself a little bit off-course, there are many ways to get back on the road to joy.

Exercise:

- Write a values statement. For example: I want to finish my degree and start working full-time in my field. I want to move across the country to California to be with my friends. I would like to start my job search there, even though most of my family lives on the East Coast.

- Examine the following list of values. Without over analyzing, circle your top 15 values.

Authenticity	Happiness	Balance	Harmony
Commitment	Health	Fitness	Compassion
Pleasure	Courage	Humor	Fun
Creativity	Kindness	Sexuality	Integrity
Excellence	Loyalty	Knowledge	Mindfulness
Family	Monogamy	Openness	Faith
Comfort	Responsibility	Friendliness	Adventure
Autonomy	Challenge	Security	Peace
Forgiveness	Humility	Contribution	Dependability
Mastery	Moderation	Justice	Inner peace
Community	Honesty	Self-acceptance	Solitude
Gratitude	Simplicity	Tradition	Stability
Appreciation of Beauty	Connection with Nature	Health	Wealth

(Note: This is short list of values. For a more comprehensive values exercise, see the resources in Appendix A.)

- Next, look at your chosen values and keep only your top ten.

- Now that you have come up with your top ten values, go back to your values statement you wrote at the beginning of this chapter. Do you see any discrepancies? Using our example, if the individual listed closeness to family, tradition, simplicity, and security, there would be some discrepancy with the stated values and the goal of moving cross-country to find a job. However, if the individual came up with such things as adventure, mastery, community, self-acceptance, and autonomy, the goal to move to California to find a job would be more in line with their chosen values set.

Some thoughts about values:

It is human nature to lose sight of our values. In other words, I may have fitness and health as a stated value, but I may sometimes forgo exercise or choose donuts over fruit in the morning. The goal of the values exploration is to help you course-correct if you find yourself straying…and we all find that we have strayed off course sometimes.

What's next?

- **Is there a value or two you have lost sight of?** This doesn't mean you have to quit your job or end your relationship this minute. There are small steps you can take to re-incorporate your stated value back into your life. For example, if you listed connection to nature as a value, but you currently live in an urban setting, set a goal to take trips to local nature preserves, parks, or city gardens over the next few weeks.

- **Keep your values in the front of your brain.** Write in your journal, share your values with a friend or a partner, and tape them to your bathroom mirror.

- **Circle back, course-correct.** Meditate on your values every morning for a few minutes. If you find yourself off track, circle back, course-correct. The good life is about learning and correcting. Even a seasoned pilot needs navigational tools to stay on course.

- **Love your contradictions.** Once you have identified your values, you are more apt to notice behavior that is contradictory. Remember that it is human nature to sometimes contradict a value. If you value health but find that you ate a lot of junk food this week, acknowledge with kindness that you have veered away from your value, and gently get back on track. In your centering journal, write down one way you will move toward that value in the next 24 hours.

- **Create a values-based mission statement instead of a goal statement** using our example above. For example: My values-based mission statement is to follow my values of adventure, mastery, and autonomy by moving to California. My hope is to build a strong community when I get there, and continue to get to know and accept myself for who I am. Share your mission statement with a close friend.

- **Explore, define, refine, and repeat!** The following exercises in this chapter give you more ideas to keep your life full of meaning and joy, even when we run into roadblocks. These exercises will help you celebrate life and love, even in times of stress, and help you to continue to fine-tune your values.

Take the Lesson, Leave the Shame

Goals:
- Understanding the difference between guilt and shame
- Letting guilt guide you, not define you

Young adulthood is a time of experimentation. Some experiments fail – miserably. These failed experiments can create a lingering feeling of shame – that awful feeling of remembering a past experiment and feeling like you want to hide under a rock. Shame serves no purpose. It is a toxic emotion. Guilt on the other hand, can be instructive. It can spur us on to be our best selves. Shame steals mindfulness. In shame it is almost impossible to be your best, loving, calm, abiding self.

Guilt says: "I've made a mistake. I own it. How can I make it right, do better next time, restore anything I've damaged, and make amends to anyone I've hurt?"

Shame says: "I am a mistake. I was born this way. I am flawed to the core. I'll never be able to make it right. I am damaged and undeserving of anything good. What is the use of aspiring toward anything?"

Exercise:

Try this centering practice this week – Consider guilt vs. shame.

- Start by taking some centering breaths. Remember to apply self-compassion when working through this exercise.

- Each day this week let go of shame by practicing the breathing for balance exercise in Chapter 5. Add the affirmation, "Breathing in, I accept support. Breathing out, I release shame."

- Work with affirmations. *I've made a mistake vs. I am a mistake* – See the difference? Many of us have been conditioned, in sometimes abusive ways, to feel shame. It can take daily work to silence the voice of shame. But mindfulness practice can help. Use your centering journal to write out a self-compassion statement. *Example: At my core I am a good person. I forgive myself for all the limitations I have placed upon myself and others. I know I was doing the best I could. I learn from experience.*

- Ask yourself, how would I act in my daily life if I believed I was a good person? How would that be different than the way I live now? Record your answers in your centering journal.

This exercise can be difficult, so keep it simple. It can bring up some tears for the harsh way we have been treated, and the harsh way we treat ourselves. Don't forget to end the exercise with the same deep breathing and check out the loving-kindness and compassion exercises in this chapter.

Making Sense of the Times in Which You Live

Goal:
- Building a sense of purpose

One way to find meaning and put your values into action is by exploring the needs of the times you live in. A side benefit of this exercise: It will help you to feel less overwhelmed by current events. Instead of feeling paralyzed by the latest doomsday news report, take some time to compare the results of your values exploration from the first exercise in this chapter and cross-reference your values and strengths with the needs of the times. For example: If you value beauty, find a conservation organization that is working to preserve a local landmark.

Exercise:

A key to happiness: Where the world's current values and your values overlap. You don't have to quit your job or change your major once you see the overlap. You can find small ways to volunteer your time or focus your efforts. You will be building self-confidence by taking action, and feel more connected to like-minded individuals as you work for causes that align with your values.

Take the following steps:

1. Think of a news story or a current event that elicits feelings of compassion or concern, or maybe has even affected you or someone close to you. *Example: I have a friend who has become caught up in the opiate epidemic. He is struggling to break free from addiction.*

211

2. Don't turn away from uncomfortable feelings, but don't let them overwhelm you either. This is mindfulness in action. You are using equanimity to notice your discomfort, but not fall into it. Breathe your way back to balance, even in the face of problematic events. *Example: My friend told his cousin that he was in recovery, she said "This is overwhelming," and stopped returning his phone calls. I'm going to make a plan to call him once a week.*

3. Once you are feeling balanced concern (otherwise known as compassion), take the next step. Ask yourself what small thing can I do to make a difference? Mother Teresa is often quoted as saying, *"We can do no great things, only small things with great love."* You don't have to be Mother Teresa to make a difference. Being of service does not require a grand gesture, or breaking the bank, or leaving yourself in a weakened position. *Example: I'm going to start looking into organizations that are addressing the opiate epidemic and find a local event that I can attend.*

4. Take action. Choose a way to take action. Many of the emerging adults I work with use volunteermatch.org, a website that allows them to commit to a one-time volunteer opportunity before making a longer commitment. *Example: There is a rally at the capital next month. I'm going to see if I can get a group of our friends to go.*

5. It's okay if you have the side-motivation to meet people. Donating your time has social benefits. Expect to meet like-minded people. If you find that the people involved with the organization are not a good fit for you, it's okay to try another group. *Example: That rally was great, but I would like to meet more people my age. I'm going to check out the local chapter of Young People in Recovery to see if they have any events.*

6. Notice how you feel after addressing the needs of the times. Most likely you are feeling more connected and less overwhelmed. Take some time to savor your good deeds.

Read not the Times. Read the Eternities.
— Henry David Thoreau.

7. Connect to other generations. The great existentialist Henry David Thoreau advised us to pay attention to eternal themes as opposed to current events. Perhaps he was encouraging us to find the mistakes that we as humans make over and over again. Perhaps he wanted us to notice our connection to humanity. What social concerns did your parents or grandparents have? What made them feel optimistic? Talk to older relatives or mentors about the social issues that concerned them when they where young. This conversation will help you see the universal and eternal state of the world, feel less isolated, and will help you stay hopeful. Write your findings in your centering journal.

Surfing the Eight Worldly Winds

Goals:
- Understanding the Buddhist construct of the Eight Worldly Winds
- Making the connection between these concepts, emotion regulation, and wise decision-making
- Using this model to stay balanced and take meaning out of the ups and downs of emerging adulthood

As we have seen throughout *Mindfulness for Emerging Adults*, both Eastern contemplative traditions and Western psychology stress the importance of regulating emotions in order to live a satisfying, happy life, maintaining balance and expressing love and compassion.

Even a happy life cannot be without a measure of darkness, and the word happy would lose its meaning if it were not balanced by sadness. It is far better to take things as they come along with patience and equanimity.

— Carl Jung

As in Jung's quote above, Buddhist thought does not distinguish between good and bad when it comes to emotions. Instead we are encouraged to master our reactions to these unavoidable states.

In Buddhism the Eight Worldly Winds represent four pairs of opposite states that everyone experiences. By acknowledging the truth of the Eight Worldly Winds we will be less apt to be blown around by them, and better able to stay in what yogis call the middle way.

Exercise:

Take some time to contemplate the Eight Worldly Winds explained below. How do they appear in your life? Awareness of these four pairs of extremes will help you flow with the breezes and the hurricanes of life. Rather then seeing them as obstacles see them as mentors, here to teach you invaluable lessons. The goal is to stay balanced even at the extremes.

1. **Gain and Loss** – We would all rather experience gain than loss, but loss happens. Loss hurts more when we are stuck in a state of clinging and grasping. Next time you experience loss, focus on generosity. Instead of what can I get ask what can I give. *Example: You lost your chance to merge in traffic because the person ahead of you would not let you in. Instead of developing road rage, can you let someone else in? How would that make you feel?*

2. **Praise and Blame** – Whether you are receiving praise or blame the trick to keeping your emotions balanced is to focus on truth. You can still feel good about a compliment, but focus on the truth and bask in your success. Likewise, focus on the truth when you are receiving feedback. This tool can even de-escalate harsh criticism. *Example: You just completed a concert with skill and precision. You are enjoying some praise after weeks of hard practice. However, your teacher is overly critical of your performance, focusing on small flaws. Instead of getting defensive or feeling crushed, listen for the truth in your teacher's statements. No truth to be found? Talk with a third party who will be honest with you.*

3. **Fame and Infamy** – Think of the rock star with a million fans one year, who is eclipsed by a new artist the next year. Hollywood therapists have many stories of the star that can't accept that he or she only had "fifteen minutes of fame." To surf the waves of fame and infamy, focus on your internal sense of self versus your external one. *Example: Last year you were chosen for a special training opportunity at work. This year, because your productivity*

215

was down, you were passed over. Resist the urge to put yourself down. Take a look at some of your successes that occurred outside of the workplace. Perhaps your productivity was lower because you chose to take family leave time to be with a sick family member or for some other legitimate reason. See the value in your actions in all life domains.

4. **Pleasure and pain** – Buddhist teachings say pain is inevitable, suffering is optional. When experiencing physical or emotional pain, be mindful of unhealthy distractions that will bring about more pain. The same goes with pleasure. *Example: You are having a yummy meal. Even though you are starting to feel full, you order two desserts. Pleasure quickly turns to pain.*

Working with the Eight Worldly Winds (each has two faces) when you are experiencing small gains and losses, will help you build resiliency and equanimity when the big winds arise.

Not Getting What You Want: Taking meaning from frustration and disappointment

Goals:
- Working with disappointment
- Recovering from setbacks

It's easier to recover from a disappointing outcome if you have had some success to fall back on. If you are an emerging adult, and you don't have a long work or relationship history, not getting what you want – a job, an apartment, a raise, an invitation, a date – can feel like a fatal punch in the gut.

But the truth of adult life is that we all face disappointment, failure, and frustration. Denying this universal truth only makes it harder to bounce back when things don't go our way. Accepting this helps us to connect with our peers in a deeper way. Accepting disappointment as a fact of life does not mean giving in or dialing back your ambitions. In fact, facing frustration and disappointment is an exercise in fearlessness. When fear is in check, we are more clear-headed and creative and better able to strategize our next move. Here's how to handle frustration and disappointment with patience and grace.

Exercise:

- **Listen for negative self-talk** – I'm a loser.... I'm a fool.... What was I thinking.... This always happens to me. Instead, talk the situation out with a trusted friend or counselor, or write down your negative thoughts and counter them with facts.
  * Instead of, This always happens to me, ask, If this is a pattern, what can I do differently next time?
  * Instead of, I'm a fool....What was I thinking? try, That

217

was brave of me to try, what did I learn?

* Instead of, This always happens to me ask, Was the timing right? Did I try to rush things?

- **Timing and patience vs. frustration** – We have all felt impatient, and there are times when we've been able to wait with ease. Which state makes you feel more peaceful? Practice patience when the stakes are low, so that you can be more patient with bigger frustrations, like a job search that is moving slowly. The next time you are not in a rush and you are standing in line, practice patience. Instead of focusing on frustration, extend compassion and patience to those around you.

- **Patience, anger, and values** – You may have noticed that impatience and anger are not on the list of values at the beginning of this chapter. What values do you hold above impatience and frustration that will help you get through your setback? Write about these values in your centering journal.

- **Patience and neuroscience** – Even if you were born with the disposition of an Energizer bunny, neuroscience tells us that we can cultivate patience with practice, and actually make physical changes to the brain. Write in your centering journal about the last time you were patient and how that made you feel.

- **Treat yourself as though you have the flu** – Have you ever heard the phrase licking your wounds? Instead of beating yourself up when you are disappointed, practice self-care. Plan some alone time or time with a trusted friend where you can be honest and open with the sadness that you feel. Don't get stuck here! The goal is to heal and integrate your experience so you can plan your next adventure. Write about a time you have experienced great sadness and came out on the other side a better person.

The Four Immeasurable Attitudes

Goals:
- Exploring four states of mind that will help you align with your values and make stronger social connections
- Appling these states of mind to everyday life

The practice of cultivating the Four Immeasurables is honored in both Buddhism and yoga and aligns with important themes in positive psychology and cognitive behavioral psychology. Using the Four Immeasurables as a mindfulness meditation practice in your daily life will foster peace of mind and positive social connection.

The Four Immeasurable Attitudes are: Equanimity, Loving-Kindness, Compassion, and Sympathetic Joy. These attitudes are considered immeasurable because of their unending ability to transform a person's life and improve the lives of others as we practice them. Each attitude is said to be an antidote to painful emotions.

Exercise:

Practice the following exercises to harness the power of The Four Immeasurables.

The practice of Equanimity: Equanimity is a state of mind that protects us from being overly judgmental, helping us respond to people and situations in a measured, thoughtful way. Practicing Equanimity helps us to react with calm to any circumstance, and protects us from the Eight Worldly Winds (see Surfing the Eight Worldly Winds earlier in this chapter). It is said to be the antidote to prejudice.
   * **Meditate on this phrase:** I strive to see all people as my brothers and sisters.

* **Use of Equanimity in daily life:** One of my roommates is easy to get along with; the other, not so much. I'll try to remember the idea of Equanimity the next time we have a house meeting.

- **The practice of Loving-kindness:** Loving-kindness is the wish that all beings be happy. It is said to be the antidote to anger, greed, and selfish love. It is almost impossible to extend Loving-kindness to others if we can't extend it to ourselves.
   * **Meditate on this phrase:** I wish for myself feelings of friendliness and Loving-kindness, I wish Loving-kindness to others around me.
   * **Use of Loving-kindness in daily life:** I am not getting along with my father. I will try to remember that he is human and trying his best. Instead of wasting my energy fighting with him, I will try to extend Loving-kindness to both of us.

- **The practice of Compassion:** Compassion asks us to stay open and present to another's suffering. Like Loving-kindness, it is important to practice self-compassion before we can share this feeling. It is said that Compassion helps alleviate fear and helps us avoid overwhelm in the face of suffering.
   * **Meditate on this phrase:** I will strive to witness my own and other's suffering, with open eyes and heart. I need not worry about fixing every problem. I will acknowledge the suffering of others, witnessing with compassion.
   * **Use of Compassion in daily life:** My friend did not get a job she really wanted. I can let her voice her disappointment. I can share my own experiences at the right time.

- **Sympathetic joy:** Celebrating the success of others allows us to also experience joy. Sympathetic joy is said to be the antidote to jealousy, envy, and depression.
  * **Meditate on this phrase:** There is an endless supply of happiness available to me. When I rejoice in my friend's happiness, I cultivate my own.
  * **Use of Sympathetic joy in daily life:** I'm so happy my friend is engaged. Extending happiness toward her helps my own levels of happiness to flourish.

- **Come back to Equanimity:** Starting and ending with Equanimity will help you develop all Four Immeasurables.
  * **Write out the following phrase and post it in a place where you will see it often:** Today I am moderate, centered and complete. I use my energy in ways that help me connect to all beings and to happiness. I treat myself and others with respect, recognizing the inherent dignity of all people.

Practicing Reverence

Goals:
- Defining reverence
- Using reverence to remember your values
- Experiencing a walking meditation to build reverence in every day life

Reverence is defined as having deep respect and appreciation for someone or something. To get an idea of how the practice of reverence might affect your mood, consider some antonyms for the word reverence like contempt, disgust or disrespect...ugh! How do those words make you feel?

Exercise:

Take a reverence walk – it's a simple practice you can try to help you feel more contentment, gratitude and well-being, right now.

- Choose a place that is familiar to you. Perhaps your home, a workspace, or a park that you visit frequently.
- Take a deep breath, making your exhale slightly longer than your inhale, emptying your torso of as much air as possible on the exhale, and noticing the split second between this exhale and your next inhale. This mindful breathing exercise will activate your parasympathetic nervous system and help reduce your stress load. Practice three complete rounds, ending with an exhale.
- Begin to walk around your chosen location. Walk slowly and mindfully enough so that you can feel the weight shifting from your left foot, to your right foot, and back again.
- Begin to look around you. Where does your eye naturally go? To the dust on a bookshelf? To a broken park bench? To a flowerbed that needs weeding? To a pile of papers

that need sorting? Know that this tendency to look for what is missing, what is out of place, is a natural human adaptation. We are wired to have an awareness of what might cause harm or be dangerous. This is a muscle your ancestors have been flexing for generations...or chances are you wouldn't be here reading this exercise!

- Consciously shift your state of displeasure at what seems dangerous or off to a state of reverence toward your surroundings. This shift toward reverence might cause you to notice a much-loved photo you pass every day but haven't really stopped to look at for quite some time. Perhaps you will notice a sofa and blanket that give you great comfort, or a flower in full bloom in the middle of a flowerbed that still needs weeding. Maybe you will notice a neighbor lovingly walking with an elderly relative through the park.

- Notice how this shift from looking for perfection to reverence affects your mood and your level of stress. Try to practice reverence for the familiar every day for the next week. Toward the end of the week, try expanding your reverence practice to include familiar people in your life.

- Do you feel more calm and content after your walk? Write a few comments about the result of your reverence walk in your centering journal.

The Meaning of Loneliness

Goals:
- Making sense of loneliness
- Managing a broken heart or the disappointment of a changing friend group

Like fear, anger, and other uncomfortable human emotions, loneliness is unavoidable. This is actually good news! Knowing that loneliness is an emotion we all feel from time-to-time will help you feel connected to the people you come into contact with on a daily basis.

Loneliness, fear, and anger also share another aspect. They are all survival emotions. Back in the time when our ancestors huddled around a campfire in the night, it was important not to stray too far. The feeling of loneliness helped us stay close to the clan, and avoid becoming a midnight snack.

Modern day loneliness is more experiential than the survival-based form, but it is just as uncomfortable. We can still use it as a cue and a tool to connect with others.

Exercise:

Here are some tips to help you harness the energy of loneliness.

- **Loneliness is a passive state.** In order to maintain loneliness, we must do nothing and connect with no one. Take action! Break free of loneliness by working through each exercise.

- **Beware of myths about being in relationships.** You may have been raised to believe that you are not whole until you are in a committed relationship. But the truth is, we can be just as lonely in a relationship as we can be when we are single. Break through loneliness by remembering what nurtures you. It might be writing, volunteering, or being in nature. Remember what makes you feel whole. Write down one or two activities you enjoyed when you were younger. Can you translate this into an adult group activity? If you loved riding a bike when you were younger, can you find a mountain biking group in your area?

- **What is good about being single?** There are pluses and minuses about being single, just as there are pluses and minuses to being in a relationship. What do you like about your singlehood? Get together with a group of single friends to brainstorm the benefits of being single.

> *"Solitude is fine but you need someone to say that solitude is fine."*
> — Honoré de Balzac

- **Don't isolate.** After noting what you like about being alone, remember that we all need human connection. Studies show that social isolation stresses the physical body and like other stressors, reduces immune function. If you have moved to a new area, or are in a friend-gap, make a pact with yourself to have some human contact every day, and a social connection at least once a week. This may mean talking to the barista when you get your morning coffee, and making a point of joining a social group, even if it means using a safe online social group until you find your true friends.

225

- **What is your self-talk about loneliness?** Watch for thoughts like I'm the only one home alone in this city on a Saturday night. What a loser. Remember that loneliness is an experience all humans share. Replace a negative thought about loneliness with one that will connect you to the human experience, such as, most people feel lonely when they move to a new place.

- **Normalize loneliness.** In our culture admitting you are lonely is like announcing you are a leper. Be counter-culture. Admit you are lonely. In doing so you are giving others permission to speak up.

- **Watch out for how social media feeds loneliness.** Many experts on loneliness believe that social media is feeding the loneliness epidemic. Remember that loneliness is not about being alone, it's one possible reaction to being alone. Be aware of how social media plays into this reaction. If scrolling through your Facebook feed is making you feel more isolated, try another social media outlet. There are many apps designed to help you meet up with like-minded friends. See Appendix A for some additional examples.

The Components of Confidence

> **Goal:**
> - Understanding the difference between self-esteem and more lasting components of identity

Self-esteem is a phrase that has been tossed around so much that it has lost definitive meaning. That is why when a young adult asks for help with his or her self-esteem, it is helpful to ask them, in their worldview what self-esteem looks like, and feels like.

Exercise:

The Components of Confidence

As it turns out there is no magic recipe for raising self-esteem. But we can look at some common factors to come up with a personalized self-esteem road map. Take a look at the following definitions and queries as a way to develop your self-esteem road map and as a means of turning the fickle state of self-esteem into the more solid trait of unshakable confidence.

- **Self-esteem** is often defined as self-respect or self-worth. Self-esteem implies a need to compare our value and self-worth in reference to group norms. We need to know what we value in order to have a more stable sense of self-esteem (see the *Center Points* values exploration in the first exercise in this chapter). Without this self-exploration, self-esteem can be shaky and can come and go, depending on external factors.
  - * **Read the following statement.** I'm feeling really good that our team met its sales goal this month. What would you say about this person's self-esteem?

- **Self-compassion,** on the other hand, is a generous, nonjudgmental acceptance of the self. Self-compassion acknowledges human vulnerability and missteps and helps us feel connected to the human race. It is a kindhearted, friendly attitude toward the self, whether or not you are meeting external goals.
  * **Read the following statement:** I'm not happy that he turned me down for coffee. Rejection is part of life though. It's okay to feel down. I know it will pass. If I can remember that this happens to everyone, I won't feel so wounded. Do you think this individual is exhibiting a helpful or harmful attitude?

- **Optimism** is another piece of the confidence puzzle. Optimism is a state of trust that even difficult situations will work out. Like self-compassion, optimism is a strength that can be developed.
  * **Read the following statement:** This assignment isn't going exactly as planned. I'm hopeful that after today's meeting we will have a better idea of how to proceed. Write your own statement about a current situation with realistic optimism. Optimism doesn't solve problems, but it can help move toward creative solutions.

- Optimism helps foster **resiliency** – the ability to bounce back from difficult situations, which in turn helps to build a sense of mastery or self-efficacy, which is one's belief in the ability to accomplish a desired task.
  * **Read the following statement:** Not having the funds to return to school this semester is frustrating. I'm going to talk to my friends who have gone through this situation to come up with a plan to get back to school. Is this a resilient way to look at the dilemma of not having enough money to return to school? Can you think of time when you were resilient? Do you have a

friend that you admire for his or her ability to bounce back? What helped them bounce back?

You may feel like some of these statements are unrealistically cheery, and depending on your circumstances, they may be! You can't control for horrible bosses, bad behavior on a date, or tuition increases. You can, however, build the capacity to be kind to yourself during set-backs, ask for help to get back on track if you are feeling discouraged, and develop a realistic optimism. By adding self-compassion to your self-esteem skills set, you will be building a lasting confidence, and a more stable sense of self-esteem.

You might also think that by being too kind to yourself, you will never reach your goals. But remember the research on self-compassion tells us that self-compassion actually builds resiliency and motivation, and therefore, stable self-esteem.

Which component of confidence is easy for you to access? Which component do you struggle with? Talk to a friend or mentor. Come up with a plan to use your strengths and shore up the areas that you find challenging. In your centering journal, write out a plan to use all the components of confidence: Self-esteem, self-compassion, optimism, and resiliency over the next month.

To Pursue or Not to Pursue: When faced with two or more choices

Goal:
- Using what you have learned about mindfulness, along with your defined values to make wise decisions

They say you can't spend the same dollar twice. This is true about our life energy, too. This doesn't mean that important life choices should fill you with terror, even early on in adulthood, when you haven't yet had much practice making many life-altering decisions. When faced with two or more options for using your precious time and energy, a mindful examination can help you clarify your motivation, and help you feel confident about your decision, no matter the outcome.

Whether you are thinking about taking a new job, starting or ending a relationship, embarking on a training program, or physically relocating, the following questions will help you with the decision-making process.

Exercise:

Visualize your two paths

As always, take some time to center yourself before answering the questions, focusing on your breath, with special attention on a full exhale before taking the next breath. Scan for and release any muscle tension, then begin:

- Picture yourself embarking on your pursuit. Do you connect with a sense of contentment, or do you feel as though you are following the plan that your culture or family has laid out for you? Write a few words about how you feel. Remember, this is not a prize-winning essay. This is a time to write from your heart, knowing you and, perhaps, someone you trust will be the only readers.

- Picture yourself embarking on your pursuit. Do you connect with a sense of contentment, or do you feel more driven by a sense of status or fame? Write a few words about how you feel.

- Picture yourself one year after embarking on your pursuit. Will supportive and like-minded people surround you? Will you feel at least partially supported and content even if you run into roadblocks? Write a few words about how you feel.

- Picture yourself two years after embarking on your pursuit. Are you following your values, or, even if your pursuit has brought you fame and success, do you need to adjust your actions? Do you still have a sense of contentment and joy, even if your pursuit did not bring you your exact desired outcome? Write a few words about how you feel.

- Now picture yourself making a different decision and going down a different road. Go through the above steps one more time and identify your level of connection, contentment and adherence to your values. Do you feel more or less content compared to the first decision? Write a few words about how you feel.

These questions are designed to help quiet distractions and build connection with your true motivation, helping you to make decisions that bring about more contentment and joy!

How to Organize a *Center Points* Book Club

Goal:
- Starting a book club to help you integrate the lessons of the past four chapters

As we saw in the last chapter, some of us love the solitude and quiet of a personal meditation space. For others, this would be a sort of torture. If you feel you learn better in community, start a *Center Points* book club to help integrate a higher level of Balance, Belonging, Focus, and Meaning.

Exercise:

To form a *Center Points* book club

- Start with a planning meeting. Get together with a few friends who are familiar with the *Center Points* model.

- Decide on the structure of the book club meetings. Once a month is usually a good time frame for emerging adults who have many other commitments.

- Make it low key and stress free. When you are recruiting members for your book club make sure to highlight the goal is stress-reduction and acceptance. The only requirement is to explore a book that has themes of Balance, Belonging, Focus, and/or Meaning.

- Consider opening and closing the meetings with a few minutes of seated meditation, mindful movement, or a quick body scan. Offer pillows and bolsters as well as chairs. Encourage members to make physical comfort a priority.

- Choose four or five titles for the first meeting with themes of mindfulness and stress-reduction, or leading a meaningful life. These books do not have to be limited to non-fiction. See the book suggestions in Appendix A for several fiction and non-fiction titles.

- Stress the goal of learning *Center Points,* not finishing the book. Make it okay to come to the meeting even if members have not finished the book.

- Once or twice a year, make it a movie club. Find a film, old or new, that helps you remember your values and the importance of Balance, Belonging, Focus and/or Meaning. See Appendix C for a list of movies that explore emerging adult themes.

- You may find that the *Center Points* Book Club is one of the highlights of your month!

Summary:

You have now completed an in-depth journey through the four *Center Points* domains of Balance, Belonging, Focus, and Meaning. These four categories represent an important set of skills that echo the needs and wants of past generations of emerging adults, and more importantly, address the concerns of modern emerging adults.

Right now, pick one tool from each of the four *Center Points* domains - Balance, Belonging, Focus, and Meaning. Make a list of four skills you will practice every day for the next 30 days. Taking 30 days to form a small but important habit often leads to big life changes. Use whatever technology – pen and paper, smartphone or computer – that will best help you keep these practices in the forefront of your mind and your heart as you go about the business of building a happy and meaningful life.

Conclusion
Beyond Emerging Adult Development:
Emerging Adult Wisdom

When defining and studying the concept of wisdom, social scientists from different cultures commonly include the following elements: cognition, defined as understanding through thought and experience; reflection, defined as the ability to assimilate experience; and compassion, defined as the ability to have concern for the well-being of others. If you have taken the *Center Points* journey, it is easy to see that building a toolbox of contemplative exercises helps in developing wisdom.

Why wisdom matters

It is said that wisdom is a gift of aging, a consolation for physical change and decline. You might say brain research confirms this adage. Research shows that as we age we use the left hemisphere of the brain more than the right. As you have learned by taking the *Center Points* journey, greater left-brain activity as seen in mindfulness practitioners is associated with more positive emotion, self-regulation, better communication, and increased moral awareness. Older brains also tend to be more efficient at pattern recognition and less reliant on the more ancient, more reactive parts of the brain than are younger brains. By working through the *Center Points* exercises, you have learned how to strengthen connections in the wisdom areas of the brain, allowing you to begin to react to even stressful situations with calm, clarity, and compassion.

A wise, less reactive, brain is a gift of aging, but it is also a gift of mindfulness. Certainly there is no substitute for years of experience. A young computer engineer can never gain the insight of a Bill Gates or Steve Jobs at the height of their career simply through contemplative practices. However, we know for sure, both from the ancient wisdom traditions and now through modern science, that contemplative practices will help ramp up left-brain activity, even in emerging adults. It is possible to cultivate youthful wisdom.

This is reason to be hopeful, even in uncertain times. In the digital age, we can accelerate the pace of just about anything, for better or worse. But we now have visual proof that we can even speed up the process of becoming wise through mindfulness-based practices. Perhaps this will translate in living the emerging adult years with less fear and isolation and more connection and joy. Is this really possible? Yes, it is! We can cultivate youthful wisdom – increasing measured cognition, developing the ability to reflect upon and integrate both positive and negative experience, and cultivating compassionate responses to life – the benefits for emerging adults, and for our world at large, are immeasurable.

Resources for Your Journey

Knowing where to turn for help and being open to receiving help are both essential skills for successful emerging adulthood. Think of it not just as a resource list, but also as a way to start important conversations with friends, mentors, and mentees. Celebrate your accomplishments while encouraging each other to address serious health concerns such as depression, addiction, poverty, and suicide just as you would talk about the ups and downs of relationship and career choices in emerging adulthood – in a matter-of-fact, compassionate manner. It's all just part of being human.

This resource list contains mainstream resources to help you through roadblocks on your journey as well as science-backed mindfulness-informed resources.

Ideas for the *Center Points* Book Club

A sampling of *Center Points* – verified reading to enhance the understanding of mindfulness, its roots, and modern uses. Many of the experts listed below have more than one publication to choose from.

Non-fiction:
Buddha's Brain: The Practical Neuroscience of Happiness, Love, and Wisdom
by Rick Hanson

Living Your Yoga: Finding the Spiritual in Everyday Life
by Judith Hanson Lasater

Wake Up To Your Life: Discovering the Buddhist Path of Attention
by Ken McLeod

The Tree of Yoga
by B. K. S. Iyengar

*The Great Work of Your Life: A Guide for the
Journey of Your True Calling*
by Stephen Cope

No Mud, No Lotus: The Art of Transforming Suffering
by Thich Nhat Hanh

Recovery 2.0: Move Beyond Addiction and Upgrade Your Life
by Tommy Rosen

Fiction:
How Yoga Works
by Michael Roach and Christie McNally

A Tale for the Time Being
by Ruth Ozeki

Breakfast with Buddha
by Roland Merullo

Siddhartha
by Hermann Hesse

Budgeting, Employment, and Other Daily Matters

Help with finances:

Society of Grownups: Online classes to help your inner adult with finances and goal-setting.
www.societyofgrownups.com

Living Wage Calculator: This project sponsored by MIT will give you an idea of the how much you need to make to live in a certain area, with or without roommates or family members.
livingwage.mit.edu

Smartphone apps to help you get in the budgeting habit:
There are budgeting apps for all types of students. Keep fine-tuning your budgeting system until it feels right for your learning style. Here are a few highly rated apps to choose from:
- Spending tracker
- Envelopes
- Mealbudget
- Mint

The Job Hunt:

The US Department of Labor: Information on employment and training as an alternative to college.
www.doleta.gov/programs/

Occupational Outlook: The occupational outlook website provides information on which careers are on the rise as well as required training and average salaries for careers.
www.bls.gov/ooh/

AmeriCorps programs offer living allowance, job training, money for college, and loan deferment in exchange for participating in volunteer work.
www.nationalservice.gov/programs/americorps

Programs for first generation college student information.
www.imfirst.org/#

Nutrition and Housing:

Friends of youth: Helps teens transition from legal minor status to legal adulthood.
www.friendsofyouth.org

Getting food stamps: Young adult use of food stamps is on the rise. Remember that basic nutrition is a precursor to achieving balance. Programs are short term for able-bodied adults but can help you through a transition period.
www.fns.usda.gov/snap/supplemental-nutrition-assistance-program-snap

Meditation Resources

Websites:

Authentic happiness: This is a website hosted by the University of Pennsylvania's Positive Psychology program. Fine-tune your knowledge about your personal strengths and values and how to put them to use in your life.
www.authentichappiness.sas.upenn.edu

The VIA institute offers character resources, with the option to purchase a detailed report on your character strengths and how to put them to work in your life.
www.viacharacter.org/www/

Sounds True exists to inspire, support, and serve personal transformation and spiritual awakening.
www.soundstrue.com/store/

Research and resources on self-compassion.
www.self-compassion.org

Programs to enhance your understanding of mindfulness and neuroscience.
www.rickhanson.net

Whole Person Associates at has a complete selection of relaxation CD's for combating stress and practicing mindfulness.
WholePerson.com

Kripalu Center for Yoga and health
www.kripalu.org

Yoga Alliance
www.yogaalliance.org

Publications:

Yoga Meditations
by Julie Lusk, MEd, E-RYT

Yoga Nidra for Complete Relaxation & Stress Relief
by Julie Lusk, MEd, E-RYT

Relaxation Scripts for Harmony, Tranquility & Serenity
edited by Donald A. Tubesing, MDiv, PhD and
Nancy Loving Tubesing, EdD

Guided Imagery for Groups
by Andrew E. Schwartz

30 Scripts for Relaxation, Imagery, & Inner Healing, Volumes 1 and 2
by Julie Lusk, MEd, E-RYT

Guided Imagery with Children
by Sarah Berkovits

Stress Relief for Kids
by Marti Belknap M.A.

Children and Stress: A handbook for parents, teachers, and therapists
by Marti Loy, PhD

Smartphone apps for yoga and meditation on-the-go:
- Buddhify
- Headspace
- Calm
- Yogaglo
- Asana Rebel

Health and Safety

National Coalition Against Domestic Violence: Get help, raise awareness, and know the warning signs and cycle of abuse. www.ncadv.org

National Suicide Prevention Lifeline: Provides chat services. 1-800-273-8255 www.suicidepreventionlifeline.org

Dial 211 to find local resources for help in crisis: health, food, shelter, job support and more. 211 is free and confidential. www.211.org

Veteran's crisis line: Offers live confidential chat services. 1-800-273-8255, text to 838255. www.veteranscrisisline.net

Alcoholics Anonymous: Free meetings around the globe including meetings specifically for young adults. www.AA.org.

Narcotics Anonymous: Narcotics Anonymous uses the 12-step program format started in AA, but with a focus on recovery from drug addiction. www.NA.org.

Young people in recovery: Community-led chapters for young people in or seeking recovery. www.youngpeopleinrecovery.org.

Recovery2.0: Honoring all paths to recovery for the big five – Drugs, alcohol, food, sex, and money – founder Tommy Rosen collaborates with experts in the fields of addiction, mindfulness, yoga, and more Tommy hosts the Recovery 2.0 Power Hour podcast found on iTunes. www.recovery2point0.com

Against the stream: A Buddhist-based recovery program that offers in-person support and audio resources. You can find the Against the Stream podcast on iTunes. www.againstthestream.org

Smartphone apps:
- Sobergrid will help you find local individuals looking for sober communities and find rides to local 12-step meetings. www.sobergrid.com.
- Aura helps you track your mood and meditate on the go.
- Insight Timer is another great app that allows you to choose meditations that help manage your mood.

Your Guide to Mindfulness-Based Cognitive Therapy is a website that helps individuals recover from mood disorders with a special focus on using mindfulness to prevent relapse. www.mbct.com

The National Alliance of Mental Illness (NAMI): One in five Americans lives with a mental health condition. NAMI provides information on treatment and support for individuals seeking healing resources, as well as support for family members. www.nami.org

Psychology Today maintains a nation-wide directory of licensed therapists searchable by city and state, as well as issue, and treatment orientation, and cost. www.psychologytoday.com

Amy Weintraub's book and website offer resources for using yoga and meditation to promote and sustain recovery including the research backing these modalities. Her excellent website offers many free resources. yogafordepression.com

The Justice Resource Institute: Provides trauma recovery resources including trauma-sensitive yoga classes. www.traumacenter.org

_____ ⋯ _____ ⋯ _____

——————————————— ··· — ··· ———————————————

Glossary

Important terms and concepts from *Mindfulness for Young Adults.*

Accelerated change: A marker of the twenty-first century that describes the exponential rate of change brought about by the digital age.

Authenticity: An identity that is based on deeply held values, and personal goals.

Autonomy: A sense of internal control of one's life processes.

Baby boomer generation: The generation born between 1946 and 1964.

Buddhism: A system of beliefs started in the Sixth Century BCE in Asia. Many modern contemplative practices and studies are based on the Buddhist concept of mindfulness.

Community: A collective of individuals, especially in the context of social values and responsibility.

Contemplative neuroscience: A multidisciplinary field of study that looks at the changes in the mind and brain resulting from mindfulness and related contemplative practices.

Contemplative practices: Practices found in every culture that share the goals of creating deeper intra and interpersonal connection and communion. In recent years researchers have been able to quantify the ability of contemplative practices to decrease stress, improve mood states, and encourage mature, thoughtful behavior. Contemplative practices include meditation and mindfulness, but also yoga and contemplative prayer as well as many other mind/body practices. Appendix D provides a full visual in the form of the Tree of Contemplative Practices.

Circling back: Using mindfulness and other contemplative exercises like Mindfulness-based therapy and journaling to resolve gaps in adult development and the maturation process.

Developmental psychology: The study of human development over the life span.

Direct experience: Experiencing of phenomena without a filter of past constructs or future worry often using the five senses as an anchor. Direct experience is similar to the concept of "flow" in Western psychology and fosters gratitude, compassion, and a sense of well-being.

Digital age: A term describing the shift from traditional industry to knowledge-based industry and the social and economic changes brought about by this change.

Digital immigrant: Someone who did not grow up with wide spread use of technology and who must acclimate to the digitally dominated culture.

Digital native: This term refers to those born post millennial into a digitally dominated culture.

Discernment: The ability to judge well.

Emerging adulthood: The period of adulthood development falling roughly between the ages of 18 and 33, in which individuals are seeking to establish independence and intimacy. This period of adult development is characterized by transition as individuals seek to establish financial independence and meaningful and stable relationships.

Flow: In positive psychology, flow is defined as a state in which an individual is completely absorbed in the task at hand, feels competent, and content.

Generation X: The generation born between 1965 and 1980.

The good life: A term used in the science of positive psychology to describe and measure the components that make life meaningful and enjoyable.

Identity: The distinguishing set of characteristics of a person that give shape to self-concept.

Interdependence: Individuals and groups depending on one another. Interdependence is a focal point in Buddhist thought, and a global fact in the digital age. Balancing autonomy and interdependence is a major theme in emerging adult development.

Intimacy/connection: Familiarity, friendship, or romantic partnership that includes a sense of trust.

Mentor: An experienced or trusted advisor who is able to empathize and connect. In *Mindfulness for Emerging Adults,* we encourage mentors to, "Be the person you needed when you were younger."

Millennial generation: The generation born between 1981 and 1998.

Mindfulness: The moment-to-moment attention to the present without judgment or reactivity.

Positive psychology: A branch of psychology that focuses on the empirical study of positive emotions, strength-based character traits, and healthy communities and institutions.

Resiliency: The capacity to recover quickly from difficulties, often aided by a strong social network and contemplating lessons learned through direct experience.

Values: Values serve as markers for what one holds as important in one's life. In positive psychology, values are seen as an important motivation to move in a certain behavioral direction.

Well-being: The state of being healthy, content, comfortable, and happy. A multi-faceted measure of health.

Yoga: A group of mind and body practices that originated in Asia. The *Center Points* model is informed by what scholars refer to as Classical Yoga, and the Eight Limbs of Classical Yoga that outline a system of healthy human development.

Terms

The *Center Points* Domains: The categories of Balance, Belonging Focus, and Meaning, provide a system of grouping mindfulness-based practices as they relate to and support the physical, social/emptional, mental, and moral self, respectively. Motivation to establish these practices as a part of daily life can be found in one or more domain.

> **Balance:** Paying attention to the physical being. "Your animal self." Attending to diet, sleep, exercise and other basic needs such as monitoring finances and balancing group and independent activities. Balance in the physical

realm requires some moderation and routine in all things in order to maximize belonging, focus and meaning.

Belonging: Building a social network that includes people and places to turn to when you need help and giving back to that network in kind. Building social connections, family, and community. Having intimate connections.

Focus: Focus is a muscle that can be exercised. It is the ability to turn back, over and over, to the task at hand. It's easier to focus when our tasks have meaning (meaning can be big or small).

Meaning: With balance, belonging, and focus firmly in place, emerging adults can begin to turn to deeper questions. A values inventory can serve as a road map on the journey to finding the good life. Finding meaning requires self-inquiry. Asking questions such as "What is my heart's deepest longing?" "What do I (not my parents, not my boss) most deeply value?"

Developmental Psychology, Contemplative Neuroscience, Positive Psychology: Western systems of health and human development. All of these systems are concerned with attention, thought and behavior, and values exploration. **Buddhism** and **Yoga** are Eastern wisdom traditions that present systems for healthy human maturation.

At the core of all these sciences from Eastern and Western traditions is **Mindfulness.** Mindfulness-based contemplative exercises range from formal seated meditation to moving meditation and mindfully and directly experiencing every-day life.

Mindfulness for Emerging Adults takes concepts from these disciplines to help individuals build an authentic identity, reach their developmental potential and create the foundations for a good life. The *Center Points* practices can be used to help reduce stress and increase life satisfaction, especially during critical adult developmental stages, like emerging adulthood, middle age/empty nest, becoming a parent, job changes and moves, retirement, and elderhood.

_____ ... _____ ... _____

Emerging Adults on Film

Forming an emerging adult film club is a fun way to explore common triumphs and struggles that arise during young adulthood.

The following list includes cinematic portrayals of emerging adulthood through the past few generations. As you watch these films, notice how social norms have changed over the last few decades. What has stayed the same? Pay attention to class, gender, and culture issues, as well as Hollywood stereotypes. Which movies speak to you on a deep level and feel authentic? The movies are organized in clusters so you can host a themed movie night. What movies would you add to this list? Do you think some belong in more than one category? Grab some popcorn and enjoy!

Addiction and recovery
Days of Wine and Roses (1962)
When a Man Loves a Woman (1994)
Trainspotting (1996)
T2: Trainspotting (2017)

Children and choice
A Summer Place (1959)
Object of Her Affection (1998)
Waitress (2007)
Obvious Child (2014)

Dating

Swingers (1996)
Kissing Jessica Stein (2002)
500 Days of Summer (2009)
He's Just Not That Into You (2009)

Divorce

When Harry Met Sally (1989)
Sweet Home Alabama (2002)
Take This Waltz (2011)
Celeste and Jesse Forever (2012)

Family

Terms of Endearment (1983)
American Beauty (1999)
Rachel Getting Married (2008)
Away we Go (2009)

Friendship

Beaches (1988)
Reality Bites (1994)
Friends with Money (2006)
Bridesmaids (2011)

Gender identity

Boys Don't Cry (1999)
Hedwig and the Angry Inch (2001)
Transamerica (2006)
Boy Meets Girl (2015)

Identity

The Graduate (1967)
Breaking Away (1979)
How to Be (2008)
Tiny Furniture (2010)

Independence

Splendor in the Grass (1961)
Harold and Maude (1971)
What's Eating Gilbert Grape (1993)
JoyLuck Club (1993)

Marriage

Guess Who's Coming to Dinner (1967)
Diner (1982)
A Walk on the Moon (1999)
Why Did I Get Married? (2007)
One Day (2011)

Mental illness

Benny and Joon (1993)
Girl Interrupted (1999)
Garden State (2004)
Silver Linings Playbook (2012)

Military service and war

The Great Santini (1979)
The Deer Hunter (1979)
1969 (1988)
Brothers (2009)

Sexual orientation

Heavenly Creatures (1994)
Brokeback Mountain (2005)
C.O.G. (2013)
Moonlight (2016)

Trauma Recovery
The War at Home (1996)
Good Will Hunting (1998)
Mysterious Skin (2005)
God Grew Tired of Us (2006)

Work and Career
Working Girl (1988)
Office Space (1999)
Adventureland (2009)
Up in the Air (2009)

——————————— ⋯ ——————————— ⋯ ———————————

The Tree of Contemplative Practices

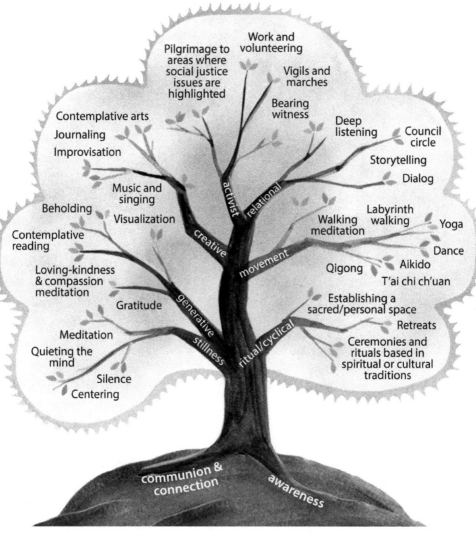

The Center for Contemplative Mind and Society

Arnett, J. J. (2014). *Emerging Adulthood: The winding road from the late teens through the twenties.* New York: Oxford University Press.

Cornish, A. (Writer). (n.d.). The Face of the Millennial Man [Television episode]. In *All Things Considered.* Retrieved from http://www.npr.org/2014/07/17/332364130/the-face-of-the-millennial-man-sketched-in-data

Crane, R., Brewer, J., Feldman, C., Kabat-Zinn, J., Santorelli, S., William, J., & Kuyken, W. (2016). What defines mindfulness-based programs? The warp and the weft. *Psychological Medicine, December.* http://dx.doi.org/10.1017/S0033291716003317

Davidson, R. (2012). Psychological effects of tai chi training. *University of Wisconsin.* Retrieved from http://journal.frontiersin.org/article/10.3389/fnhum.2014.00013/full.

Epstein, M. (2013). *Thoughts without a thinker.* New York: Basic Books.

Friedman, T. L. (2016, November 2). Donald Trump Voters, Just Hear Me Out. *New York Times,* Opinion Pages. Retrieved from https://www.nytimes.com/2016/11/02/opinion/donald-trump-voters-just-hear-me-out.html?smid=fb-share.&_r=0

Greeson, J. M., Juberg, M. K., Maytan, M., James, K., & Rogers, H. (2015). A randomized controlled trial of Koru: A mindfulness program for college students and other emerging adults. *Journal of American College health,* (May). http://dx.doi.org/10.1080/07448481.2014.887571

Hendrikson, C., & Galston, W. A. (2016, November 21). [How millennials voted this election]. Retrieved March 1, 2017, from brookings.edu website: https://www.brookings.edu/blog/fixgov/2016/11/21/how-millennials-voted/

Hölzel, B. K., Carmody, J., Vangel, M., Congleton, C., Yerramsetti, S. M., Gard, T., & Lazar, S. W. (2011). Mindfulness practice leads to increases in regional brain gray matter density. *Psychiatry Research: Neuroimaging,* 191(August), 36-43. Retrieved from http://www.umassmed.edu/uploadedFiles/cfm2/Psychiatry_Resarch_Mindfulness.pdf

McGonigal, K. (n.d.). *The neuroscience of change: A compassion-based program for personal transformation* [Audio tape]. Louisville, CO: Sounds True. (May, 2012)

McLeod, K. (2002). *Wake up to your life: Discovering the Buddhist path of attention.* New York: HarperOne.

Millennials in Adulthood: Detached from institutions, networked with friends. (2014, March 7). Retrieved March 1, 2017, from Pewsocialtrends.org website: http://www.pewsocialtrends.org/files/2014/03/2014-03-07_generations-report-version-for-web.pdf

Pepping, C. A., Hanisch, M., Zimmer-Gembeck, M. J., & O'Donovan, A. (2014). Is emotion regulation the process underlying the relationship between low mindfulness and psychosocial distress? *Australian Journal of Psychology,* (March). Retrieved from http://onlinelibrary.wiley.com/wol1/doi/10.1111/ajpy.12050/abstract

Phil, J., Christopher, P. A., & Halford, W. K. (2015). Individual differences in dispositional mindfulness and initial romantic attraction: A speed dating experiment. *Personality and Individual Differences,* 82(August). http://dx.doi.org/10.1016/j.paid.2015.02.025

Quaglia, J., Goodman, R., & Warren Brown, K. (2014). From mindful attention to social connection: The key role of emotion regulation. *Cognition and Emotion,* (December), from http://www.tandfonline.com/doi/abs/10.1080/02699931.2014.988124.

Shaw, H. (2013). *Sticking Points: How to get 4 generations working together in 12 places they come apart.* Carol Stream, IL: Tyndale House Publishers, Inc.

Solman, P. (Writer). (n.d.). Are the best days of the U.S. economy over? [Television episode]. In *PBS Newshour.* Retrieved from http://www.pbs.org/newshour/bb/are-the-best-days-of-the-u-s-economy-over/

Vaillant, G. (2012). *Triumphs of Experience: The men of the Harvard Grant study.* Cambridge, MA: Belknap Press.

Weintraub, A. (2003). *Yoga for depression: A compassionate guide to relieve suffering through yoga.* New York: Harmony.

Weintraub, A. (2012). *Yoga skills for therapists.* New York: Norton.

Woolery, A., Myers, H., Sternleib, B., & Lonnie, Z. (2004). A yoga intervention for young adults with elevated levels of depression. Alternative *Therapies in Health and Medicine,* 10(Mar/April), 60-63. Retrieved from http://www.modernhcp.com/INNO-PDFS/IMCJ-PDFS/BE8EAF15F08842A291DC88418F8F9BA5.ashx.pdf

WholePerson

Whole Person Associates is the leading publisher of training resources for professionals who empower people to create and maintain healthy lifestyles. Our creative resources will help you work effectively with your clients in the areas of stress management, wellness promotion, mental health, and life skills.

Please visit us at our web site: **WholePerson.com**. You can check out our entire line of products, place an order, request our print catalog, and sign up for our monthly special notifications.

Whole Person Associates
800-247-6789
Books@WholePerson.com

CPSIA information can be obtained
at www.ICGtesting.com
Printed in the USA
FFHW012323280519
52706624-58213FF

9 781570 253539